Alexander Johnstone Wilson

Reciprocity, Bi-Metallism, and Land-Tenure Reform

Alexander Johnstone Wilson

Reciprocity, Bi-Metallism, and Land-Tenure Reform

ISBN/EAN: 9783337295325

Printed in Europe, USA, Canada, Australia, Japan

Cover: Foto ©Suzi / pixelio.de

More available books at **www.hansebooks.com**

RECIPROCITY, BI-METALLISM,

AND

LAND-TENURE REFORM.

BY

ALEXANDER J. WILSON,

AUTHOR OF "THE RESOURCES OF MODERN COUNTRIES," "BANKING REFORM," ETC.

London:
MACMILLAN AND CO.
1880.

The Right of Translation and Reproduction is Reserved.

PREFACE.

THE greater part of the following chapters on "Reciprocity" appeared in *Macmillan's Magazine* early in the year. Want of space then prevented the writer from discussing the question of land reform, and an attempt is now made to fill the gap thus left. It is still however but an outline; the writer naturally feeling that a subject so thoroughly handled in all its bearings by the many competent writers who have preceded him gave no excuse for detailed reiteration of threadbare arguments. The chapter on Bi-metallism has been added for the sake of completeness. That remedy for dull trade has been nearly as much in vogue as "reciprocity" with many people, and, along with "reciprocity" and the re-imposition of corn duties, it exhibits that curious outburst of trades-unionism among the moneyed classes which a time of languishing trade has produced. There is consequently a unity of design in the following pages which may not at first blush appear. The subjects treated in it are either various phases of one and the same disease, or the remedies which that disease requires. For much that the writer has put forward under the latter head he expects little thanks from many. Although conscious of a desire to suggest the means of averting revolution he will probably be told that his remedies are worse than the disease.

But if the existence of the disease be recognised much will be gained, and should what follows help to quicken public apprehension on that point, the writer will be well satisfied. The diseases of the body politic, once recognised and understood, will themselves force the application of remedies; and however much in love with an abstract theory he may be, yet on the question of practical remedies the writer is quite content to take his stand amongst the opportunists.

LONDON, *December*, 1879.

CONTENTS.

CHAPTER I.

                                                                                              PAGE

CAN RECIPROCITY HELP US?—THE GENERAL ANSWER TO THE QUESTION 1

CHAPTER II.

THE FUTILITY OF THE RECIPROCITARIAN PROPOSALS . . . 51

CHAPTER III.

SOME MINOR LESSONS OF THE PRESENT TRADE DEPRESSION . 78

CHAPTER IV.

THE GOSPEL OF BI-METALLISM 106

CHAPTER V.

THE EFFECT OF AMERICAN COMPETITION ON BRITISH AGRICULTURE AND BRITISH LAND LAWS . . . 153

CHAPTER VI.

RADICAL CURES FOR THE EVILS OF FEUDALISM 193

CHAPTER VII.

THE REMEDIES OF EXPEDIENCY AND COMPROMISE 232

POSTSCRIPT 253

RECIPROCITY, BI-METALLISM,

AND

LAND-TENURE REFORM.

CHAPTER I.

CAN RECIPROCITY HELP US?—THE GENERAL ANSWER TO THE QUESTION.

FEW things have lately been calculated to oppress the mind more heavily than the troubled state of English industries and the confused ideas to which that state has given rise. Men wont to face their difficulties manfully, seem to have given way to a kind of despair, and clutch wildly at whatever promises a quick and easy way out of their distress. Prominent and influential sections of the nation are to all appearance disposed to apply palliatives to the situation, which can only aggravate their difficulties. If there be a principle of political economy which one might have sworn was fixed in the English mind never to be shaken, it is the principle of "free trade." Men of all shades of political opinion vied with each other in its praise. Free trade was like a new revelation, and the very squires themselves hesitatingly joined in boasting of what it had done to make England great. They might not, any more than the masses, have other than the haziest conception of what the words "free trade" meant, or of why the thing they represented should be so good; but the cry was fashionable, and more than that, the rents of land had risen in an unprecedented degree since the new era began. So dinners were given in honour of the new faith, and the flow of eloquence heard at these dinners and on all public occasions indicated clearly that free trade was firmly rooted in the hearts of the people. With that faith held high, we should yet subdue the earth. Already the triumphs to which it had led us exceeded those of ancient Rome. We had an empire on which the sun never set, and our ships traded to every known region of the globe. Before our merchants and manufacturers, opponents melted away like snow at the touch of spring, and all by the might of free trade. Listening to pæans chanted in a lofty strain like this, a stranger might have been forgiven for thinking that to an Englishman "free trade" was something holy—a faith never to be parted with—dearer to his heart than all the Christian creeds.

Less than three years ago he was a bold man who would have dared to doubt the absolute soundness of this mercantile principle; and the man who could sneer with effect at our neighbours still in the bonds of protectionism was always sure of applause. Three short years ago! and now what do we find? We find that a large and increasing section of the working classes and of the trading community, as well as a most important proportion of the owners of land, are roundly asserting that this free trade has been all a mistake. "We have gone on the wrong principle altogether, and shall be ruined if we do not retrace our steps." When you ask these people what they want, they do not speak very clearly, it is true, but that probably arises from shamefacedness. Many of them have been such ardent wordy free-traders in the past that they cannot at once veer round and loudly abuse their old love; so they prevaricate. They declare that "in theory, you know, free trade is an excellent thing—so excellent, that practically it will only work in the millennium! In these merely human days the world must content itself with something less perfect, lower if you will, but more practicable and handy." The cry, in short, is "Free trade in theory, but in practice Reciprocity!" That is the new word which is going to charm back to us all our waning prosperity. As yet only a word, we may soon expect to find it a political cry, and unless the country is wiser than it has lately shown itself to be, from a cry it will probably pass into a living, working policy.

Many things combine to make this contingency less remote than it seemed but a few months ago. First of all the Government wants money—a great deal of money, as is the custom of Tory Governments; secondly, the landlords want to maintain their rents, at last threatened by the action of free trade, superadded to bad harvests; thirdly, many of the farmers are not unlikely to say that they want the same thing as the landlords; and, finally, the manufacturer and shipper want a larger foreign trade, which they seem in many cases to imagine "reciprocity" will give them. The change that a few years of dull business has wrought upon the ideas of the trading and moneyed classes is indeed astounding. Men now advocate what they before cried down, and as beaten children run to their mothers for shelter and comfort, these "reciprocitarians" come running to parliament for assistance against the aggressive foreigner. In this feeling the workmen join the manufacturers much as the farmers join the landlords. A well-informed correspondent, writing to me from Manchester—that cradle of the free-trade movement—gives the following account of the state of mind existing there now upon this question :—

"It is a great mistake to suppose that the mass of the people of this country are free-traders from intelligent conviction. They are nothing of the sort. The bulk of the working men, whatever they may call themselves, are protectionists. So also are very many of the merchants and manufacturers. These latter almost all say that they are free-traders, but when they come to explain, they are not free-traders, unless 'the people we deal with are free-traders too.' I talk with no end of such people. 'You see,' they say, 'what your free trade has brought us to at last.' 'And are you not a free-trader?' I ask. The usual reply is, 'Oh, yes; I'm a free-trader in the abstract—of course everybody is that now; but I don't think it works well all round.'

"This is the state of mind very common at present among the younger merchants and manufacturers here, and it will certainly be turned to account at the next general election. Of course nobody will go in for 'protection in the abstract;' but there will be much sneering at 'ultra free-traders'—at 'men who, not content with ruining our industry and prosperity by over-production at home, insist on exposing us to the mad and reckless competition of the whole world,' &c., &c. That such talk is meaningless, or destitute of definite meaning, instead of being any objection to its acceptance, is only a ground for believing that it will go down the more sweetly."

This is a very disturbing account of the thoughts prevailing in the leading manufacturing centre of the country. The "hard times" are obviously producing an unlooked-for effect upon the weaklings of the present generation, and the nation may yet have to fight its free-trade battles over again. To a free-trader by intelligent conviction that seems hardly possible, but we must never forget that the world is not governed by intelligent convictions. Stupidity is still, alas! a most powerful factor in mundane affairs, and the more stupid a people is, the more easily will it follow a mere sound. You might turn "Tweedledum" into a capital political cry if you contrived to make believe that it meant higher wages and more beer.

It was shrewdly remarked by Mr. Horace White, of Chicago, at the recent Cobden Club dinner, that the English had been converted to free trade through their stomachs, and the remark was only too true. For a while it answered most marvellously in filling empty stomachs, but a new generation has grown up, crowding the towns; new conditions are coming to the fore such as try the feeble faith of those who thought that the summit of human progress had been attained. In spite of free trade, "hunger" has once more appeared among us, and what its presence may convert us to Heaven only knows.

It is therefore time to take a look at this generation's new pet trade-reviver. What do these adversity and hunger-driven people mean? They say, "Love free trade platonically, but use something else for every-day purposes." We must seriously endeavour to discern what that something is. For fear one might be accused of misrepresentation, it will be best to give the description in the words of some of those who obviously consider themselves chosen apostles of the new sect. Take this as a first sample:—

"The most ardent free-trading theorist would, I suppose, be ready to agree with me that the protective tariffs of foreign nations and in some of our own colonies are injurious to the manufacturing interests of Great Britain. But I am prepared to go much further than this, because I entirely believe that those protective tariffs, if continued long enough, are not merely injurious to our home industries, but will come to mean the absolute extinction—so far as manufactures are concerned—of our export trade. Nor do I think that foreign nations or the colonies are at all likely, of their own accord, to modify those tariffs to our advantage. I say deliberately 'to our advantage,' because I believe that protectionist nations are not such fools as our British political economists would have us believe them to be. It seems to me that these foreign and colonial gentlemen for the most part understand their own interests perfectly, and that we may reason with them until Doomsday without any result so far as the advancement of free-trade principles is concerned. They will adopt free trade if free trade suits them; and, for the most part, our friends are perfectly able to judge, without any assistance from us, whether free trade does or does not suit them. In plain truth, our British political economists—those who are our teachers—fail to understand that the laws of trade include elements which their theories have not yet grasped. Certain things ought to be, according to theory, which nevertheless are not, so-called political economy to the contrary notwithstanding. Our teachers have, I think, still something to learn; but, as it seems to me, it is at least quite clear that free-trade theories have in practice completely broken down. My business friends tell me it is not the fact that American commerce is as depressed as our own. I am assured also that French commerce is fairly prosperous, and that even in Russia trade is better than with us. I know of no British industry that is really active except the making of machinery for export to those who find it more remunerative to manufacture abroad.

"I am not against free trade. I want to see reciprocity in trade; but I do not believe we shall ever get it by talking political economy to our trading competitors. Foreign nations have less to gain from free trade than we have. It is a matter of business; and if we want real free trade—as assuredly we do—we must go beyond the present teaching of British political economy and make it the interest of those who now exclude our manufactures to adopt a different policy. Our foreign friends who decline to understand the advantages that free trade offers would understand at once the disadvantages under which a British retaliatory tariff would place them. Those to whom I am opposed on such questions say sometimes, I think unreasonably, that retaliatory tariffs to be effectual must be prohibitory. They say also, but I think only with partial truth, that we could only levy duties upon articles of food; and they put forward as an axiom, I think upon insufficient data, that the entire cost of all such taxation would be borne by the British consumer. But it can easily be shown that retaliatory tariffs far short of anything prohibitive would, in many instances, 'turn the scale' in favour of purchasing from such nations as might be willing to accept British manufactures in payment for their productions. I think, also, that we are none the richer as a nation by continuing to import inferior French watches in Hall-marked cases, although the vendors who sell them as of British manufacture may become so; nor are we much the better for getting such things as French silks free of duty when we cannot export woollens or cottons or anything else of home manufacture in return, And if, in the absence of a retaliatory tariff, we do get some of our sugar a little cheaper than would otherwise be the case, we are, I think, paying too dearly for such cheapness in submitting to the extinction of British sugar-refining. But even a tax upon imported grain, unless universal, need not injuriously affect the consumer.

Some portion of the burden would no doubt fall upon him, but some also upon the foreign producer. The foreigner would have to content himself with smaller profits; our untaxed grain-exporting colonies would be gainers in finding a better home market for their wares; and the consumer, able to pay in kind, could better afford to buy.

"We ought, as it seems to me, to face our national position in a business-like way, as any business man would in his own affairs; to realise that in adopting free trade without reciprocity, a mistake has been made, and that our path cannot be too soon retraced. Once admit the principle that retaliatory tariffs may lawfully be used 'as a means to an end,' and there need be no difficulty in again finding markets for British manufactures, nor in so working our fiscal system as to strengthen the commercial ties with those magnificent colonies which I trust may long form with Great Britain one great united Empire."

So says Mr. David MacIver, M.P. for Birkenhead, in the *Times* of 16th Nov. 1878. We cannot complain that his utterance is hesitating. He laughs the theorists in political economy to scorn, tells them that they have yet something to learn, that free trade has completely broken down in practice; and, not content with that, boldly announces that reciprocity is the sovereign remedy for the decline of our trade. We want real free trade "assuredly," but we cannot have it till other nations come to think as we do, and in order that they may speedily so come, we must punish them a little. "Our foreign friends who decline to understand the advantages that free trade offers would understand at once the disadvantages under which a British retaliatory tariff would place them." Here you have the whole secret. Reciprocity means retaliation. We are to preach free trade as the followers of Mahomet preached Islamism, by a little forcible persuasion. If nations became converts to a new creed by the power of the sword, why not to a new political idea by the might of retaliation? According to Mr. MacIver's policy—and he expresses the feelings of thousands of influential people at this moment—we are to say to our colonies, "Give up your protective tariffs, or we will shut out your raw produce." To the French we must say, "None of your wines can come here unless you take in exchange our linen, woollen, and cotton goods, to any extent we choose to send them." To the United States the message would be, "Take our iron and machinery, our manufactured tissues and our ships, or keep your bread and cotton to yourselves." One can imagine under this retaliatory system our customs' officers telling the people of Victoria, say, that they must remove their 50s. duty on iron under pain of having to submit here to a duty of 10s. an ounce on their gold, or 2s. a cwt. on their wool. And so it would be all round. The customs' tariff that would meet on their own ground the various nations with whom we are thus to trade would be the most remarkable ever devised. It would embody a sliding scale on a new principle, according to which duties would be high or low in proportion as those of the countries upon whom we were "retaliating" were high or low.

This I take to be the meaning of these "reciprocity" ideas, and that I have given no travesty of them is proved by the utterances of another prominent exponent of the new faith. Lord Bateman, who has written and spoken more on the subject than even Mr. MacIver, managed to get a debate raised in the House of Lords, in April last on our free-trade policy. In opening that debate he delivered a clever and very ingenious speech couched in terms of a much less hoity-toity tone than the letter just quoted. But substantially it came to the same thing. His plea was that we could have no "one-sided" free trade. Such a thing was a delusion and and a misnomer, and we were therefore all on the wrong tack. "We had," he said, "for a long time past been throwing away in the most gratuitous manner many millions sterling of customs' duties which had been either repealed or reduced simply as sops to the free-traders or as occasional sops to disarm opposition." And then he proceeded to give his definition of reciprocity, which is as follows :—[1]

"His own definition of reciprocity was that it was not necessarily protection, and that it was in reality mutual interchange and barter for the benefit of both parties. They had reciprocity of feeling in love (laughter), and the only thing in which there was not reciprocity was in commercial affairs. He did not ask for protection, but he contended that if there were no reciprocity there could be no free trade. Reciprocity ought to be regarded as the coping-stone of the free-trade system. It was the one thing wanting to the establishment of that universal free trade which every one desired, but which had not yet been secured. He would illustrate the meaning of reciprocity by referring to the duties on tea. Out of the four millions raised by the duties on tea, one million was derived from our own Indian empire. Now, the other day we had remitted 200,000*l.* of cotton duties—that is to say, we made the Indian empire pay 1,000,000*l.* on tea and 200,000*l.* for the cotton imported from this country. This was unfair. If we had done away with the 200,000*l.* on cotton and had at the same time relieved our empire from the million that was derived from tea, we should have been illustrating the principle of reciprocity. But it might be asked, what was his idea of reciprocity—how did he propose to carry it out? (Hear, hear.) Well, in the first place, he would propose a close federation between England and her Colonies in all

[1] *Vide Times* report, April 30th, 1879.

parts of the world, establishing between them free trade in the most unrestricted sense. In New Zealand there were hundreds of thousands of quarters of wheat annually used as manure or thrown into the sea simply because California being nearer to this country than New Zealand, the New Zealander found it impossible to send his wheat to us under present circumstances at a profit. That was not a state of things which ought to exist. Again, could anything be more disastrous or more painful to witness than the position occupied by Canada at the present moment? There was no doubt that the Canadian tariff would act most injuriously on the trade of this country, and it was by no means certain that the colony of Victoria would not follow suit. There was no cohesion between the Mother Country and its dependencies such as ought to exist. We relied upon foreign imports and shut out entirely our own colonies from trading with us. Under the system he proposed every scrap of import duty on colonial produce would be abolished, and the result, he believed, would be that we should be able to snap our fingers at all foreign countries, being no longer dependent upon them. A small deficiency of revenue would, of course, have to be met, but it might easily be made up by a tax upon intoxicating liquors, which would at the same time have a beneficial effect upon the country by diminishing drunkenness. If that were not enough, some other small indirect tax might be levied. He was advocating, not protection, but reciprocity, which meant a mutual exchange of benefits. They should urge it upon all foreign nations, and if those foreign nations accepted it they would enter into the federation of which he had spoken. If they refused it, the question of import duties would of course arise. But he did not wish to talk about protection. He did not wish to mention the word. At the same time he would admit that, in his opinion, if foreign nations would not accept the principle of reciprocity, we ought, by way of inducing them to do it, to impose a certain small restriction —he did not care how small—on foreign imports."

The childlike hopelessly muddle-headed adroitness of this is most admirable. There is no thought of protection, of course not; "we only want a free-trade federation. First, between this country and her dependencies; then, between ourselves and foreign countries." And no dream could be more beautiful. But supposing the colonies and these other countries refuse to listen to the voice of the charmer? Ah! then a little gentle pressure must be put on, just a pinch of customs' duties by way of reminder and to further conversion. Thus it comes in the end to the same thing as the fisticuffs and swagger of the other apostle, or of the German Bismarck. If mutual free trade does not spring up at our bidding, then we must win it by force—the force of persuasive retaliatory tariffs. We must, in short, give blow for blow and triumph by a process of exhaustion. Such ideas as these surely require only to be brought to the test of practical life to stand revealed in their natural absurdity. The promulgators of these notions of course disclaim so rough an interpretation. They tell us that they want nothing so extravagant, only, as Lord Bateman gently puts it, just a taste of what protective tariffs mean, administered as a wholesome corrective all round. If they mean that, why not say so at once, and honestly? Why wrap up protection, under the guise of "reciprocity" or "retaliation," trying thereby to palm off on the people as a new and sovereign specific what is really an old and exploded quack dodge? Protection is at least something tangible, which "reciprocity," whether in its maudlin or its truculent guise, is not. You could no more punish other nations for not adopting free trade, by treating each according to the measure of its protectionist iniquity, on its refusal to re-arrange its fiscal system at your bidding, than you could prevent the earth turning on its axis. The world has grown too big for such nonsense, and were powerful nations to be treated in this fashion by us, they would simply laugh at us, and take their trade elsewhere. America, for example, would find no difficulty in disposing of its cotton in Europe were we to shut it out from our ports by a retaliatory duty. No doubt Europe would be very happy to take our place in supplying the eastern and other markets with the manufactured tissues made from that cotton.

We must not, however, dismiss these notions lightly because they are nonsensical, for the circumstances of the time favour the ascendancy of folly. There is no denying that the country has lost some of its foreign trade, that competition increases abroad and misery at home. These facts are patent enough, and the distress of many here makes the wildest proposals of relief find eager acceptance. The new "reciprocity" cry is therefore a serious affair, and must be treated seriously.

The "retaliation" people are mostly to be found amongst the trading and manufacturing classes, while the protectionists proper are mostly in the ranks of the landowners. These two classes may possibly join their forces with a view to obtain legislation in the direction of their fancied interests; and as a practical outcome of their agitation we may live to see protection once more established—at first, perhaps, tentatively, but possibly with increasing vigour, as its mischiefs develop themselves.

Mr. MacIver's letter—to which I revert because it is so frank and clear—indicates with a brusque contemptuous definiteness the line of argument which is likely to be adopted by such a reactionary party, and the sophistry of it is in a measure sheltered behind the self-assurance with which assumptions are stated as axioms. He denies boldly, for example, that the only taxes we can impose would be on raw materials and food, and is equally sceptical of the effects which import duties on manufactured articles, supposing them effective, would have on the British consumer. He even goes so far as to assert that a tax on imported grain need not injuriously affect the consumer; and, in short, throughout his letter, laughs the accepted and *proved* maxims of political economy to scorn.

Political economists will no doubt say that argument is wasted on such peoople. And so it is: but still the nonsense has to be faced, for the sake of those who, though ignorant, are open to reasonable conviction, and for the sake of the nation which may be led astray by this will-o'-the-wisp. And I take Mr. MacIver's letter as the most pronounced and conspicuous type of the stupidity which prevails on this subject. His assertions are useful, in so far as they give a clue to the mischiefs which foolish people would bring down on the nation if they could.

There are several ways by which the core of the question may be reached, and the difficulty is to choose the simplest. On the whole, it seems best that the subject should be met less by the advance of theoretical propositions than by an appeal to facts, and to the facts I shall therefore as much as possible address myself. Those who wish for a clear statement of the principles of free trade as applied to the present situation of affairs cannot do better than read Mr. Fawcett's recent volume on *Free Trade and Protection*.[1] Protectionists, too, might be much benefited by a perusal of Chapters V. and VI. of that work, which deal specially with the evil effects of high tariffs and with the causes that produce hostility to existing commercial treaties.

Mr. MacIver touches with very great skill upon those few facts which seem most to favour his notions. He mentions, as I shall show, only those industries which bulk largely in the figures of our import trade, and those nations alone who claim to be prosperous. In so doing, however, he omits some most essential considerations, and in order to bring the points of the debate sharply and clearly before the mind of the reader, it will be well so to divide the subject as to secure a fair review of the facts. Admitting to the full the recent decline of our trade, it shall be my object to show by citations of facts regarding the industries of other countries that protective duties give no security against decline or stagnation in their case. The ground to be gone over in this way is very extensive, but the investigation need not be very minute.

[1] Macmillan & Co.

Enough is known about the general condition of foreign countries to make the task of determining the economic value of this trade policy comparatively easy. This part of the subject may be termed the negative demonstration of the folly of protection, or its twin sister reciprocity. But the negative demonstration is not sufficient. It will likewise be necessary to prove that the remedy for our distress advocated by the reactionaries is one that we could not apply, however legitimate it may be. We must show that the nation has taken a step which cannot safely be retraced. Under free trade a form of national existence has grown up in these islands which we cannot with impunity now cut down or train into new forms; not only so, but the characteristics of our foreign trade may now be such as to make any attempt at throttling other nations by a retaliatory tariff on their manufactures ludicrously impotent. While dealing with this part of the subject it will also be useful to examine the proposals and theories of those who find the cause of all our present ills in the state of the currency. Bi-metallists are not exactly protectionists, but they advocate a peculiar form of reciprocity, and are therefore within the scope of this discussion, and it shall be my task to try and prove that their—what may be called—homœopathic cure is as little likely to help us as any other.

But supposing all this proved, the reciprocity party may fairly say, "How then will you deal with the national distress?" That it exists is admitted on all hands, and it must certainly be alleviated; and I shall be prepared to suggest a remedy. Instead of deserting free trade at the first pinch of adversity it may be well to consider how much more widely the principle can be applied at home. The landowners and many foolish farmers, want, for example, to re-impose taxes on food. Suppose that instead of doing so we were to remove the obstructions from our land, and so increase its cultivation and yield. That is an ultimatum no doubt dreaded by the land-owning class, but its interests are remote and insignificant compared with those of a work-needing and perhaps hungry nation, and the alternative is therefore one that the reciprocity party and their allies must face. We must discuss it therefore, and with it sundry subsidiary remedies, all tending, as I hope, to aid the nation in bearing its present strain.

The range of inquiry thus briefly indicated is tolerably extensive, and its parts are not easily separated. To some extent they may overlap each other, but it shall be my effort to avoid both repetition and tediousness as much as possible. With this by way of introduction we shall now proceed.

A review of the prevailing state of manufactures all over the world must necessarily be very brief, but I hope it may not prove less conclusive upon that ground. The thing to do, however, is to exhibit in all its naked significance the alarming decline in the value of our own export of manufactured goods, and this will be done most readily by the following table, which gives the average figures of these exports at three distinct periods, beginning with 1863-65. The first two periods may be considered periods of inflation, and the last one of depression :—

Exports.	Average of years 1863—1865.	Average of years 1871—1873.	Average of years 1875—1877.
Cotton yarn	£9,163,000	£15,884,000	£13,383,000
,, manufactures	44,082,000	60,898,000	56,831,000
Linen manufactures	7,946,000	7,678,000	6,243,000
Steam engines and other machinery	4,831,000	8,062,000	7,664,000
Iron and steel	15,127,000	33,284,000	22,199,000
Silk manufactures	1,429,000	2,041,000	1,658,000
Woollen and worsted yarn	5,054,000	5,868,000	4,375,000
Woollen and worsted manufactures	18,076,000	28,305,000	19,202,000
Total	£105,708,000	£162,020,000	£131,555,000

If we take the figures of our total exports of home produce—nearly all of which, except coal and coke, represent manufactures of some kind—the results are not much more cheering, the averages being 157,000,000*l.*, 245,000,000*l.*, and 208,000,000*l.*, for the respective periods. There is thus, however we take it, a heavy falling off in our export trade, and the year 1878 even gave no indication of improvement. On the contrary, the figures were lower than the average of the previous three years or than that of 1877, being only 193,000,000*l.* And the current year (1879) tells almost the same story. Trade has shrunk more, and the credit of our merchants has become strained to an extent that has made a few American iron-orders like gifts from Heaven.

The full weight, however, of these figures, and of this steady decline in the export of British and Irish produce, cannot be estimated without taking into account the import trade. That up to 1878, instead of decreasing, increased at a very rapid pace. And in 1878 itself the excess of imports over exports of home produce was about 181,000,000*l.*, or 82·3 per cent, although the imports exhibited a falling fall amounting to 7·2 per cent. compared with the total of 1877. After deducting the value of foreign goods re-exported, there was still a difference apparently against this country of 128,185,000*l.*, or an excess of 47 per cent of imports over the total exports, bullion included.[1] Such a huge divergence would seem to afford grounds for the alarm

---

[1] *Vide* the 23rd Report of the Commissioners of H.M. Customs, p. 8.

excited in the breasts of the reciprocity party, and justify the cry that the country will be ruined by buying too much, if something is not done to restrain it. To such a cry it may well be replied (1) that the country is in no great danger of continuing long to buy what it cannot pay for, and (2) that within limits the apparently excessive buying may in the circumstances be the most profitable trade we can do.

Still the divergence between the values of our import and export trades has been increasing in recent years, and must be taken note of. Had there, however, been no severe and persistent decline in the values of our exports, it is not likely that the cry of distress would have been raised by the reciprocitarians on this or any other ground. That is where the shoe really pinches.

Ever since 1873 prices have been falling, from a variety of causes, until they are in some instances upwards of 50 per cent lower than they then were. In 1873, for instance, the average value of pig-iron was nearly 6l. 5s. per ton. It was lately below 2l. 10s., and some kinds of Cleveland brands were selling at less than 40s. per ton. This is an extreme instance, approached only by the fall in coals and copper; but we must make allowance for a more or less analogous fall in prices all down the list before we can definitely estimate how we stand. Quantities have in some cases fallen severely, undoubtedly, but not as a rule to the degree which the fall in values would lead us to suppose; and great as the relapse has been, we are not yet, as regards even the value of our exports, nearly down to the level of the early part of last decade.

A paper lately read by Mr. Robert Giffen before the Statistical Society deals very ably with this point.[1] I am quite unable to endorse all that he says, because I think he allows mere figures and isolated facts to sway his judgment to the exclusion of many other important considerations. Still there is a great deal in what he urges, as I shall have occasion to try to explain. He makes, it appears to me, far too much of the functions of the precious metals in the present crisis; and in dwelling on the fact that our export trade, measured by its bulk, has been stationary rather than declining, he seems to miss the full force of one highly important characteristic of the troubles through which we are passing. The present trade crisis has not been of that abrupt continuity-breaking type with which previous crises have made us familiar. Partly, perhaps, because of the enormous reserve wealth possessed by our manufacturing classes, there has been a continuance of

[1] Vide *Journal of the Statistical Society*, for March, 1879.

production in many departments of trade long after the returns obtained might have warned producers to stop. We are thus probably suffering from a slow exhaustion of our manufacturing capital, instead of a sudden collapse; and the continuance of heavy exports in the face of steadily diminishing prices is, from this point of view, a far worse sign than a sharp general contraction would have been. So, doubtless, the protectionists interpret it. They feel that the maintenance of trade under present conditions is steadily leading to ruin, but instead of pausing, they continue both production and consumption upon an excessive scale, and turn round on the nation, demanding that it should tax itself to secure them profits in spite of their own folly. The grievance is not what Mr. MacIver represents it to be. We are not, except in the particular direction where his experience lies, exporting less; our export trade gives no signs of dying out. On the contrary, its volume is nearly as large as ever, but its profitableness has nearly disappeared.

When prices give way rapidly, as those of the iron and coal trades have done since 1873, while production at the same time continues on a large scale, the result is almost sure to be a steady accumulation of losses. Year after year weak firms which have struggled against adverse fates, producing what they could not sell at a profit or at all, and thereby increasing the depression of a market overweighted without them, see themselves forced into bankruptcy. They go on and on till debt and ruin overwhelm them. This is what has been done in this country, and we saw last winter part of the results of it in distress or starvation throughout the land. What then grieved and alarmed many may be again upon us in a form yet more alarming, because the same process of exhaustion has continued. Social want and misery still exist to an extent probably never before known in this country at a time when bread was cheap. It might have been better for the capitalist, and better for the bankers who have too frequently taken the place of the capitalist, had the prolonged crisis, marked by the downward course of prices, been sharper, for then it would perhaps have been over long ago. But it has not been sharp. On the contrary, it has dragged us slowly downwards, till many have been ready to despair because of the suffering which a lengthened period of trade depression has entailed.

From one point of view therefore the fact that quantities and values have shrunk in very unequal degrees, rather aggravates than lessens the discomfort and loss of the " dull times." We have been in some cases generously enriching our neighbours by selling them goods under cost price. That is clearly very bad business; but admitting it to be so, what has that to do with protection, reciprocity, or anything else except a natural and inevitable law? The tendency of mankind is to run to extremes; and some years ago we ran to an extreme of production and of cost of production which has now brought its legitimate and inevitable reaction. A man opened a coal-mine and found it pay. Forthwith he mortgaged it and opened with borrowed money half-a-dozen more. While the years or months of an inflated prosperity lasted he called himself rich, and perhaps bought himself a landed estate which he also mortgaged. This went joyously forward till prices shrank and demand fell off, when he at once found himself over head and ears in debt, without a farthing in the world that he could call his own. So with manufacturers of all kinds. They rushed deeper and deeper into a career of unlimited production on borrowed capital—thus artificially stimulating consumption—and must now sadly learn the lesson that the sole duty of mankind is not to buy china-clayed cottons, "shoddy woollens," or steam-engines "at maker's prices," with other people's money.

This kind of business enterprise has gone on here, and has gone on more or less abroad; but we must not confound it with the "over-production" complained of by the working classes. Inflation, in the sense of enormous extension of credit ventures, has too often been accompanied by actual reduction in the amount of work done by a given number of hands. This point will, however, be more appropriately discussed at a later stage. It is in the meantime necessary to find out how other countries fare who "protect" themselves from the evils of free trade.

The United States, Mr. MacIver hears, are prosperous, and his news is, in a general way, correct. But in what are they prosperous? Certainly not in their manufactures. They have been feeding us while we laboured at forge and weaving-frame; and we have bought their corn and cotton so lavishly, that all United States agriculturists are in a fair way to be rich; but the manufacturing industries of the Union have been struggling for years under depression as deep as our own. I find, for instance, by a recent report of the American Iron and Steel Association, that in the year 1877 the number of old blast furnaces abandoned almost equalled the number of new ones constructed, and that of 716 furnaces in existence, only 476 were in blast. There was no sign of improvement during 1878, and I believe that a still further reduction then took place. Capital continued during that year to be lost in these undertakings—a good deal of it English capital; prices continued to sink, and wages have been so reduced that ironworkers and miners have the greatest difficulty in maintaining existence. The home make of pig-iron has fallen off almost uninterruptedly since 1873, and the disorganisation of the American iron trade has been fully as great as our own. In spite of a protective tariff of unusual severity, the prices of American pig-iron have sunk as steadily as ours. In 1873 the average price per ton was about 8*l*. 12*s*.; in 1877 it was only 3*l*. 16*s*.; and in the end of last year it was barely 3*l*. There have, no doubt, been special causes at work in the States inducing a fall in quotations, amongst which we must give the chief place to the gradual "appreciation" of the paper dollar; but we cannot be sure that the rise in value of American paper has not affected this country also to a very large extent, and, whether or not, this one fact stands out prominently, that the iron trade of the States has not been made profitable by means of a protective tariff. At the date of this writing steel rails can be bought in Middlesborough for 4*l*. 15*s*. per ton, while their price in the States is about 8*l*. 14*s*. The duty charged on English rails imported is 5*l*. 10*s*. per ton, or about 120 per cent on the lowest English prices, yet that duty barely saves the makers of the States from being beaten by us, and while it prevents the United

States consumers from benefiting by our lower prices, does not render their native trade prosperous. It may be said that the iron trade is no fair criterion, since it has been revolutionised by the invention of new and simple processes for making steel. These inventions no doubt complicate matters, but the complication affects us just as much as it does the States, and their tariff does not help them one whit. Their manufacturers get nearly twice the prices current at Middlesborough for their steel rails, and yet cannot make a profit. As for having an export trade of large dimensions to relieve the internal pressure, that is clearly an impossibility; we can undersell them to any extent. It may, however, be urged that since the end of last year this industry has greatly improved within the Union. Glowing accounts come to us through the newspapers, setting forth the renewed prosperity which has arisen in the industries of the country. And in a certain sense these statements are of course true. There has been renewed activity during 1879 in the American iron trade, but that renewal does not imply prosperity by any means. On the contrary, it is merely the sign of a fresh outburst of speculative inflation. Such inflation has overtaken everything American since the New Year, and the secret of it is to be found in the legal resumption of specie payments. There has been no actual, or only a very microscopic actual, return to specie payments under the resumption law, and its main effect has therefore been to distend credit. As soon as this distension has reached its limit, reaction, and not improbably collapse, will again set in, and we shall then see what the "revival of activity in the United States iron trade" really means. In the meantime, and to be generously fair, let credit be given for what has actually been accomplished.

There has been recently a considerable revival of trade and speculation in the States, and the prices and production of pig-iron have both increased. Already, in fact, theirs have risen to the competing level, and English iron and steel are being imported into the States at a profit, tariff notwithstanding. The tariff thus protects only up to a certain point. Directly this point is passed foreign competition becomes again effective, and paves the way for a renewed collapse in the native industries by presently underselling native producers in their own markets. The tariff sends up cost of production at home until the home industries become choked thereby.

The condition of the United States cotton and woollen manufactures is not any better secured. Throughout we have the same story, dragging prices, and either no profit at all, or very reduced profits. More money has been lost in the United States in efforts to develop these industries, than would have sufficed to develop the agricultural resources of one of their largest Territories. People embark in mills and machinery, lose their money, and sell their property to a fresh set of adventurers at ruinous loss. These, in turn, struggle for a few years, and then, in a great number of instances, also succumb. It is true that there are a few conspicuous exceptions, but these have either remarkable advantages in the shape of special machinery or water power, or they make a kind of cloth which the Americans put up with as the best they can afford while debarred from importing better goods. The ordinary American manufactures, both cotton and woollen, are far inferior in quality to the higher makes of English goods, while the isolated position of the industry, coupled with the disastrous competition within a limited area, inevitably tends to lower the standard of business honesty. In this respect the woollen trade seems to be worse than the cotton, though by far the most "protected" of the two. But all these American industries are highly "protected," and as a result their "prosperity," when it does fully come, is of a very precarious kind, as it surely must be so long as the cost of every manufactured article is higher than it is here by from 50 to 150 per cent. In other words, the American people pay this tax for the privilege of wearing home-made goods of inferior quality, but costing extravagant sums, and in order that a few persons in the States may have a precarious chance of making a fortune.

This, without exaggeration, is the net upshot of protection in the United States, and as a proof of its futility against the industries of England it should be stated that the Americans infinitely prefer the fine English woollen cloths to those of their own country. They still import English broad cloths, for example, although they pay about 140 per cent. duty on them; and no American comes to Europe without taking home as many clothes of English make as he can decently smuggle through the Custom-house. Add to this the fact that, as we shall see later on, protection has never enabled the States to build up an export trade worth mentioning in manufactures, and we have a tolerably strong practical proof that retaliation is not the potent medicine for the distressed manufacturers of England which reciprocitarians make it out to be. The fact of the matter is, that we have been hearing a great deal too much of late about the wonderful progress of the United States as a manufacturing country. Its prosperity is based almost entirely on its marvellous agricultural development. Stop that development, and reduce the profits of American agriculturists by keener competition or greater production in Europe, and above all in England—and the manufacturing industries of the States would, if still protected, almost perish. As it is, they languish rather than flourish. With all the aid of a rigorous tariff, the States are not yet self-contained, nor have the numerous advantages secured by the invention of ingenious machinery placed them in a position to be our rivals outside their own borders. To understand fully the actual state of the textile and other industries of the Union, we must remember that the economic conditions of production are not altogether the same there as they are in this country, or in Europe. By reason of the extent and richness of their soil, and of the ease with which its cultivation can be taken up, the people of the United States can at present afford to pay for the luxuries of native industries a price that no old European country can stand. Viewed in relation to her capacity in this direction, the marvel is, not that the States have not yet established their textile industries on a secure basis, but that they have not swept us from the field. Their cheap food alone should have given them an inestimable advantage over us, but it has not yet done so. Their progress has in short been in spite of their tariff, not because of it, and the position now gained can only be kept at a sacrifice which the people of the States are every year growing less willing to bear. More than once since the Civil War, want has overtaken the industrial population of the United States in spite of cheap food and an almost limitless territory, and had Europe had the happiness of enjoying bountiful harvests instead of bad ones since 1875, there would have been a condition of prostration manifested to-day by the United States that would have been a spectacle to the world. Her tariff would have disappeared before the clamours of a needy democracy.

We must therefore treat the United States as in some measure a country apart. For a time the inevitable effects of a selfish, grasping, and exclusive trade policy may be obscured there by exceptional circumstances. An internal prosperity may be visible, and industries appear to flourish, but sooner or later the true effects will reveal themselves. But even if they did nothing of the kind, granting that the spurt visible in the Union since January 1879 has an enduring character, it would not avail the "reciprocitarians," for the simple reason that it is not based on prosperity in the export of manufactures. That is the source of our prosperity, not selfish exclusiveness; and if the United States tariff proves anything, it surely proves to demonstration that articles manufactured under it are sure of no extensive market outside the tariff "ring fence."

Proof of this statement will be given when we come to deal with the question of the practical application of retaliation by England. In the meantime we shall find fully as strong evidence of the futility of the tariff remedy for bad trade, or its uselessness as a trade creator amongst nations, at our own doors.

France, for example, has had for nearly twenty years a comparatively mild import tariff, but before 1860 it was one of the most cumbrous and exclusive in Europe. It was nearly as bad, in short, as the United States tariff is now, and, but that the French navigation laws were less barbaric than those of the States, would have been quite as bad. The French ought therefore to have then felt the blessings of retaliation or protection, and to be now lamenting their folly in becoming less exclusive. They are, in fact, lamenting; and at the present time the cry of many French manufacturers is that they are being ruined by English competition. For instance, Messrs. Ellison and Co. state in their annual review of the cotton trade, published in October, 1878 (a most admirable publication), that their French correspondent writes to them as follows: "If England, in the face of the development of the cotton industry in all parts of the world is not able to find a new outlet for her manufactures, and does not reduce her immense production, our industry is destined to be ruined next season." That is a most alarming prediction, and we are happy to say that it has not yet been fulfilled. Yet there can be no denying that the values of French exports of manufactured goods do not tend to increase any more than our own. On the contrary, they have of late years been, like our own, steadily diminishing. The figures are of course not nearly so low as they were before 1860; but they are lower for cotton, silk, and woollen manufactures than they were on the average in the first half of the decade following that date. The inference of the French manufacturer therefore is, that France has not enough protection. Her general trade has benefited prodigiously by the loosening of her bonds in 1860, but certain special manufactures have not of late years maintained their earlier level. Hence many of her manufacturers want to revert to the old policy of exclusiveness, and this just raises the point which I should like our reciprocitarians to settle. Where is the line of retaliation to be drawn? If a little pinch of imposts does not revive trade, can a big dose thereof be guaranteed to do so? The United States, with a monstrous load of protective and prohibitory duties on their back, do not get along so well outside their own borders as France with a much lighter burden; but France also, though less weighted, feels the backwardness of the times—where in these circumstances is the happy mean to be found? Will special remedies cure an evil that pervades the trade of all countries in a great measure irrespective of their tariffs? Do we want to shut ourselves within our own borders? and if so, who will then feed us? If not, what on earth are we to do? I confess questions like these puzzle me much. For it is notorious that France has taken immense strides as a manufacturing country since she adopted a comparatively liberal policy in 1860. That unfettering was like a resurrection to her, and all the losses caused by the accursed war of 1870-71 have not been able to destroy the good thus obtained. Are we in the face of a broad fact like this to accept the new cry of the distressed Frenchman suffering from the same blight as ourselves, and believe that what was so good during the last seventeen years is now to be instantly discarded? This is what Lord Bateman, Mr. MacIver, and their followers apparently want us to do. But can they explain why a good which everybody recognised yesterday should to-day have become an evil?

The truth of the matter is, that we have had far more to fear from French competition since 1860 than we ever have had to fear from America. And in spite of bad times we shall continue to have more to fear so long as France does not follow the example of the "blood and iron" campaigner of Germany and go groping for help and wisdom among the dead and buried fallacies of a barbaric past. We must not, in plain terms, disguise from ourselves the too obvious fact that the French are still prosperous, notwithstanding the wailings of a few Frenchmen who may not be making the profits they would like. Their agricultural interests are on the whole flourishing, and their export and import trade has increased very much since 1860. They have of late years bôught more raw material for making up at home, and have sold enormously increased quantities of home products for consumption abroad. In spite of their tariff we are, it seems, able to beat them in some kinds of cotton goods, but they hold their own against us and against the world in the manufacture of the finer kinds of light woollen fabrics. This superiority may be due to their merino wool, and the skill which long custom has given to their artisans in weaving it; but whatever its cause, the fact must be acknowledged. Yet their trade has, it seems, lately paid badly in these fine fabrics as well as in silk goods. These latter, however, they have adulterated to an extent which puts the feats of our enterprising cotton-spoiling rogues quite in the shade, so that we might, in this instance, say the tariff had nothing to do with the decline. But in other cases the comparatively light tariff which formerly acted like a charm in extending French trade has clearly not prevented temporarily reduced prices, losses, and so forth, and if it cannot prevent a fall in France, how is it to induce a recovery here?

A most remarkable fact in connection with the lamentable prophecy of Messrs. Ellison & Co.'s French correspondent deserves to be noticed before we go further. He wants "more protection" against these terrible English; but when we turn to the figures of English exports of cotton goods to France, we find that they have actually been falling off for some years, both in quantity and value. This applies not only to cotton piece goods, but likewise to woollen piece goods, and, in a less degree, to silk and woollen yarns. The only articles of British manufacture which are sustained in quantity are cotton yarn, and linen yarn, and piece goods. The values of machinery and of wrought and unwrought iron are also pretty well sustained, but in the one class of article against which we have quoted so strong an outcry for more protection, there is decidedly less trade doing than there was in 1874, or for that matter five years earlier. The higher import of cotton yarn, perhaps, explains this anomaly, for the French spinners have a special grievance against us. In a memorial which they recently presented to a commission appointed by the Chamber of Deputies to examine into the state of French industries, they tried to make out that the cost of producing French yarn was about double that of English yarn— 89 centimes per half kilo against 46 centimes—and they accordingly demand a "countervailing" duty. This estimate is, I believe, a pure work of the imagination, and the real cause of the steady import of English yarn into France is to be found in our superiority as spinners of cotton. We can beat the French in the finer kinds of that product, just as they beat us in certain departments of woollen manufacture; so they buy our fine yarns notwithstanding the present duty of 15 or 20 per cent. I shall touch on the "cost of production" question further on, but in the meantime it may be sufficient if I support my assertion on this point by pointing to the fact that the French imports of raw cotton have of late years been largely on the increase. This proves that their spinning must be on the increase also, as in fact it is. They have become able to supply the home market with the commoner kinds of cotton fabrics, which they can manufacture throughout at home. In time, perhaps, their increased skill and improved machinery may enable them to overtake us in the production of the finer qualities of thread and webs, but their tariff is certainly no help to them in the race. Even now it does not cause an increase in their trade abroad, and all practical experience teaches that the higher you raise a protective tariff, the more surely you prevent the growth of an export trade in large industrial products.

Much might be said about the industries of other European countries, but the reader would weary of the same story over and over again. The briefest possible summary must therefore suffice. Mr. MacIver very cleverly cited Russia in support of his thesis, and there can be no question that the industries of Russia have lately been in a way prosperous, and that too after a great rise in her customs tariff. But if you examine the facts you will find that it has been an entirely delusive prosperity, due to the enormous depreciation of the paper rouble, a depreciation which makes the trader think he is realising large profits. By and by he will find out his mistake, just as the United States manufacturers have done, high tariffs and government bonuses notwithstanding. Germany has a considerable export trade, but it is of a very fitful, disorganised, and altogether muddled kind, owing to the burst of insanity which came over the German race after its successes in the war with France. So unsatisfactory and unprofitable has German foreign trade proved in recent years, that the German manufacturers have petitioned Prince Bismarck to give them what the manufacturers are clamouring for here. Ever since January 1877, to take but one example, the German iron producers have been moaning out the familiar song, "We are ruined by English competition," and all because the small import duty on pig-iron had been abolished. That song is a favourite one everywhere abroad just now, and is set to precisely the same music as the English dirge, "We are ruined by foreign protection." The facts are oddly against the Germans in this instance, for we have not sent them so much iron since the duty was taken off as before. They suffer from their poverty, their miserable resources, and their wild ambition; but England makes a good scapegoat, and Prince Bismarck decided to gratify the wishes of the clamourers in the true spirit of Lord Bateman and Mr. MacIver. At one time this brilliant political campaigner leant to the free traders, but that mattered nothing. Principles have nothing to do with government in the mind of a man like Bismarck, for to him politics are a game. There are "points" to win, enemies to crush, personal aims to be gratified, and from before these public right quite as much as true economic principles must perforce stand aside. For my part I am delighted to think that Prince Bismarck, in his anxiety to consolidate his spic-and-span new German empire, has decided to try a protective tariff as the cure for its languid industries and socialistic troubles. "Better Germany than ourselves," even if for no other reason than that in some respects the Germans are further from freedom than we are. The scorpion's whip of protection applied to the people there is likely to hasten the breaking of the chains which Bismarck and his master have ingeniously forged for the purpose of keeping the nation in their grasp. I anticipate, in short, some curious manifestations of social disorder and political impatience as an early fruit of the Prince's new departure. That he is marching straight to destruction, though with the confidence of a man of many victories, I make no doubt. The condition of Germany, before the imposition of this grotesquely-conceived tariff of Prince Bismarck's, proves, in spite of drawbacks, that more was to be gained by free trade than by protection. Under a liberal tariff some of her industries were slowly recovering. What they will do under the new law is not difficult to guess.

Trade has been dull in Germany from causes

easy to specify and unconnected with tariffs, just as in other European countries. Trade, in short, has been dull everywhere, tariff or no tariff; wages have fallen, strikes have broken out, banks have failed more or less frequently, in all countries possessed of industries worth naming. Even quiet-going Sweden has not escaped a crisis, loss, and much depression. Wander were you will the story is the same, and it would be the height of folly not to recognise the universality of the facts. The recognition, however, is fatal to the assumptions of reciprocitarians. And so is the other broad fact, that on the whole those nations whose tariffs are as a rule the lowest, are the best able to compete against the manufactures of England in neutral markets. As I shall have to show in the next chapter, countries with prohibitory tariffs do not compete in any real sense at all, whereas a country like France, whose woollen manufactures alone are estimated to be worth about 50,000,000*l.* a year, has increased in competing power more or less steadily for years. And so it has been with other countries, such as Germany, Holland, and Belgium.

The converse of this is also true, viz., that high tariffs do not mean the effectual exclusion of foreign manufactures from the countries where they exist.

As examples of this we may take the figures relating to the United States and Spain given in the excellent annual statement of trade issued by our Custom House. These tell us that in 1877, in spite of the high tariffs, we sent to the States cotton fabrics to the value of 2,447,000*l.*, and woollen fabrics to the value of 1,728,000*l.* True, these figures show a great falling off compared with those of five years before, especially as regards woollen goods; but that is no proof that the tariff *per se* is beating us, for the tariff was just as high when we sent 6,000,000*l.* worth of these goods as when we sent less than 2,000,000*l.* worth. It would be just as legitimate a conclusion to say that the States must have been very much poorer in 1877 than in 1873, or that prices must have been very much higher then than now, as to say that protection is destroying the English power of competition. Our real power of competition with the States is in point of fact greater now than it was five years ago, and should trade recover we ought to beat them as they never yet have been beaten.

Our trade with Spain is far more insignificant than with the States, and her tariff has been recently raised very much to our disadvantage; still the old one was rigorous enough, and in spite of it our export of cotton cloths and woollens to Spain has been year by year increasing. The export of silks also increased materially in 1876 and 1877, and our hardwares, linens, and metals have been, all things considered, wonderfully well sustained. So much is this the case, that comparing 1877 with 1873, the total export of home manufactures to Spain shows a falling off of only 100,000*l.* on a total of 3,637,000*l.*, and that notwithstanding the severe fall in prices which has occurred in the interval.

These are but one or two examples of the futility of protective tariffs as a means of excluding foreign goods; they might be multiplied almost indefinitely.

Can we say that these facts go to help the protectionists?—our revengeful distressed capitalists? I repeat that I should like them to tell us how. Without some higher aid than has been yet developed there is no discovering the advantages of reciprocity. But ample evidence is to be found that protective tariffs always mean diseased industries. In a time of inflation they fail to keep out foreign goods; they merely raise the cost of production, and also perhaps —though that by no means follows—the profits on production, to a fabulous level. High profits and wages induce altogether abnormal developments of particular industries. Capital and men rush into the favoured trade, and then when reaction comes, and there are no more high profits or wages to be had, they find themselves stranded. Their commitments and the high cost at which they produce effectually shut them out of neutral markets, and so they set about preying upon each other within their own borders. "Protected" manufacturers thus become the "Kilkenny cats" of trade, and consume each other unpitied.

Are we going to enter upon such a career for the sake of giving immediate relief to our distressed capitalists? Is the nation as a whole to be expected to pay higher prices for its clothes, its tools, its locomotion, its almost every "necessary," in order to save capitalists who may have plunged too deeply into a career of adventure and reckless outlay from the effects of their own imprudence? I trust not; but at all events we may be sure, that whether the nation consents to do this or not, we have no ground in the experience of other nations for supposing that the last state of the manufacturers under protection would be better than the first under free trade. There is no evidence that high custom tariffs help weak industries to make a profit in time of general depression, still less that they contribute to the maintenance of a competitive trade. Negatively, therefore, the case against reciprocity seems to me to be complete. When we ask what good tariffs in protection of manufacturers have done, there is no satisfactory answer. The highest tariffs in existence do not prevent competition from without, or stave off ruin from within.

CHAPTER II.

THE FUTILITY OF THE RECIPROCITARIAN PROPOSALS.

In a general and negative way the futility of protective tariffs as trade revivers has been proved in the previous chapter. We examined there the position of industries in some of the principal manufacturing countries of the world, and found nowhere proof that they had got any good by their tariffs. In each instance where a certain kind of prosperity was visible notwithstanding those tariffs, it could easily be traced to special circumstances wholly apart from anything a protective tariff could do. Thus in the case of the United States we found that the misfortunes of Europe had been a source of great gain to their agriculturists, and that artificial resumption of specie payments had led to a burst of wild speculation, so producing a temporary glare of prosperity. In France and Germany both, dull trade had come when tariffs were low, and yet both were more prosperous than when tariffs were high. Special causes were likewise at work in Russia, and there was therefore fair ground for coming to the conclusion that fiscal legislation, designed no matter how cunningly, could not help our own country out of her troubles. So, too, customs duties, however high, had no distinct power even to destroy competition from without. All depends on the capacity of the buyer to pay. If that is small, high customs duties will extinguish home industries as well as crush out foreign competition; while, if it be high, foreign goods will be just as readily bought at high prices as home-made. In this way the conclusion is reached that, however help may come to us, it cannot reach us through a customs tariff drawn up in imitation of that of the United States or of Prince Bismarck, or even of Canada.

That, however, is but one side of the question. If we turn back to the utterances of Mr. David MacIver, or listen to those of his way of speaking, we find that the immediate object of the imposition of reciprocity duties in this country is not the improvement of our own trade so much as the economic well-being of our neighbours and rivals. Our new economic sect is filled with an overmastering pity for the benighted heathens of protection in other lands, and they propose that we should convert them to free trade by means of a protective tariff of our own. That looks like a quixotic kind of operation at the best, but we must nevertheless accept the statement. Reciprocity in self-torture must be adopted till the nations learn to make free trade "work well all round."

So only half the case has been proved by a demonstration of the futility of protection as a trade reviver. We are going to set an heroic example in order that our neighbours may learn; and what matters it if, in punishing them for their obstinate heresy, we ourselves suffer loss? For the general good much ought to be endured. The question comes then to be—To what extent can we in the first place punish the adventurous competitive manufacturers of other countries by the imposition of duties on such of their goods as find their way here?

To answer this question briefly I must inflict on the reader a few more figures. The extent of our import of foreign manufactured goods must be ascertained before we can judge of the force and efficacy of the punishment which the reciprocity people propose to administer. It is the foreign manufacturer who is our great enemy, and in all fairness he ought to be the first to suffer punishment. We shall therefore take the figures of the imports of foreign manufacturers over the same period as shown in the previous table, and see where the lash of retaliation can be successfully applied. The last year indicated in this table is the *maximum* point of our import trade :—

IMPORTS OF FOREIGN MANUFACTURES.

	Average of years 1863—1865.	Average of years 1871—1873.	Average of years 1875—1877.
Stearine candles . . .	£166,000	£348,000	£362,000
Clocks	248,000	413,000	453,000
Cotton manufactures .	876,000	1,496,000	1,618,000
Artificial flowers . . .	305,000	409,000	542,000
Glass	540,000	1,221,000	1,462,000
Leather gloves . . .	990,000	1,340,000	1,930,000
Iron and steel, manufactured or wrought . .	389,000	948,000	1,462,000
Zinc manufactures . .	197,000	301,000	422,000
Paper	368,000	526,000	558,000
Silk manufactures of Europe	7,420,000	9,036,000	12,068,000
Refined sugar and candy	1,147,000	3,319,000	4,750,000
Watches	250,000	409,000	468,000
Woollen manufactures .	1,851,000	4,174,000	4,822,000
Woollen yarn for weaving	973,000	1,325,000	1,469,000
TOTAL . . .	£15,720,000	£25,265,000	£32,386,000

Taken as they stand, these figures, which include almost every article of importance, certainly show remarkable progress. The second period, as compared with the first, exhibits an increase of fully 60 per cent. The last period, as compared with the second, gives an increase of only 28 per cent; but then the lapse of time between the two is much smaller.

Altogether, in comparing the first period with the last, the increase in our imports of foreign manufactures here enumerated has been fully 105 per cent. Nor is this all. There is a large number of small articles not distinguished separately which have also to be counted. The exact value of these articles cannot be given, but the total of unenumerated articles imported has risen in value from 17,227,000*l*. in 1865, to 37,954,000*l*. in 1877, and it is therefore fair to assume that whatever proportion of manufactures may go to form this total has contributed its full share to the increase.

In many instances also values are now much lower than they were five years ago, or twelve years ago, so that the figures here set forth—the only ones we can give—do not, as a rule, really show the extent to which foreign manufactures are competing with our own. Just as our own exports have not fallen away in bulk nearly so much as they have in value, so our imports of foreign manufactures have not increased in value at the same rate as they have increased in bulk. This may be proved by one or two percentages. Woollen yarn, for example, has risen in the quantity imported by fully 189 per cent since 1863-65, while the value has only grown about 163 per cent. We have no means of comparing the quantities and values of silk manufactures imported, but from the great amount of cheap or adulterated silks which have lately been sent to this country, it is fair to assume that the same divergence, or even a much greater divergence, is also to be found in these. And we can, at all events, note this fact—that while the value of silk manufactures imported has been steadily augmenting of late years, our imports of raw silk have with equal steadiness fallen away. In 1863-65, we imported on the average 7,603,000 lbs. of raw silk per annum; in 1871-73, this average had fallen to 7,333,000 lbs.; and in 1875-77, to 4,982,000 lbs. Here again, however, we must observe that our export of raw silk has been very much less of late years than it used to be, so that the actual consumption of silk in this country would not appear to have fallen off to the extent these averages would lead one to suppose. It has fallen off nevertheless, and the falling off must be faithfully recorded. Still even here we must not forget that special causes are at work. Fashion, and the debasement of silk manufacturing by the French system of adulteration, have doubtless much to do with the disorganisation of our home manufactures, and so far it is certainly not a matter for remedy by the imposition of duties.

Turning next to refined sugar, we find that the average imports of the three periods we have chosen for comparison are respectively, 688,000 cwts.,

1,881,000 cwts., and 3,029,000 cwts. This gives an increase in the first period as compared with the last of 340 per cent, while the values for the same periods give an increase of but 314 per cent. The contrast is greater still between the figures of the second and third periods, during which the quantity has increased by 64 per cent, while its value has risen only 43 per cent. Our import of refined sugar is therefore increasing at a very rapid rate, a rate that much outstrips the increase in the import of raw sugar, which has barely been 53 per cent since 1863-65. Here again there are special circumstances to be taken account of in the shape of foreign bounties, by means of which France and Holland in particular are, now that no duty is imposed by us, able to beat English refiners in this country, and the sugar-refiners here have been agitating, ever since Sir Stafford Northcote abolished the sugar duties, for special protection against these bounties. They call their remedy "countervailing" duties, and seek to pass it off as something altogether different from either "protection" or "reciprocity," although it is designed to do exactly the same for the refiner that either of these quack medicines is upheld to do for other distressed industries. Its object is to make refined sugar dearer in order that English refiners may live, and it is therefore protection. As protection, it would be just as useless and just as mischievous to the country as any other provision to secure a monopoly. If the French and Dutch are foolish enough to tax themselves heavily in order to supply other nations with cheap sugar, I do not see why they should not be allowed to reap the fruits of their folly to the full. A few people in this country suffer in a temporary way because of that misplaced generosity, but the nation as a whole gains something by the bounty which French and Dutch tax-payers choose to put in the pockets of a few wealthy refiners. Probably the best way to cure these nations of their folly is to let them enjoy the payment of this half million or million sterling—nobody is quite sure of the exact amount—for a few years longer. We certainly could not cure them by the imposition of a countervailing duty, because—excluding the probability that the interested parties in these nations would in return seek revenge on us—the stoppage of the import of refined sugar would at once reduce the burden of bounties on the French and other foreign tax-payers. Until our sugar duties were abolished, they did not know what these bounties meant, but they are beginning now to do so, and will feel the pinch increasingly with every increase of the export of refined sugar from France and Holland. Therefore even these special circumstances do not justify a recurrence to protection in the shape of "countervailing" sugar duties. It may possibly have been a mistake—although I by no means grant that it was so—to sweep the old duties away, but there is no ground for their re-imposition in the circumstances urged by our sugar-refiners; and if they are re-imposed it must simply be on the ground that Tory extravagance has left the nation no alternative.

Now in the table given above, there are but three articles—woollen and silk manufactures and refined sugar—which bulk largely enough to be worth taxing at all. Of what use would it be to put a tax on any article of import which does not stand for 2,000,000*l.* a year in accounts which have amounted in the aggregate of late years to from 370,000,000*l.* to 395,000,000*l.*? For the purposes of protection such duties could be of little avail, and for purposes of punishment or retaliation they would be ludicrously inefficient. And in these three articles there are actually but two countries whose commerce would be affected by the imposition of duties here. France and Holland might be "punished" if we shut out their woollen and silk fabrics and their sugar, but no other country would be sensibly touched. Is it worth while to embark upon a course of retaliation for the mere purpose of whipping one or two nations into the sound free-trade faith? Or could the whipping thus bestowed be warranted to produce that effect? The present tendency of the trading classes in France is perhaps rather towards protection than towards free trade, and there is every reason to suppose that any adoption on our part of a protective tariff would intensify that tendency. The two countries might very soon come to hurl import duties at each other in the same spirit which dictated the First Napoleon's edicts for the exclusion of England from the commerce of Europe, and who could say that we should be the gainers in the strife? Those who argue for strife in trade between nations certainly overlook the influences of those natural causes, already spoken of, which may always be trusted to cure excessive profusion as well as excessive depression. For a number of years, ever since 1873, the United States, to take the most conspicuous example, have been buying less and less of foreign manufactures. The increase in home producing capacity was, I must again point out, not alone the cause of their doing so. They were pinched by a poverty which told on home industries far more disastrously than on foreign. But of late they have grown passing rich—both naturally and through distension of credit. And, as an immediate consequence of this augmentation of wealth, they have begun to be again greater buyers of foreign goods. They first of all took home, and often at high prices, large amounts of their debts, corporate and national, held abroad; and that accomplished, they have now begun to buy more foreign, and especially British, manufactures. This must obviously be the result of the possession of more means, no matter how acquired, for when all goods, home or foreign, are dear to them through the action of the tariff, it is a matter of comparative indifference to the wealthy whether they buy home-made products or foreign. Quality, not price, will then guide their selection.

What is thus true of the United States is equally true with ourselves, only we are getting rather poorer instead of richer. Our poverty will therefore tell, and is even now telling, in our imports of foreign manufactures and luxuries. We are perforce driven to buy larger quantities of foreign food, and these cause the totals of our imports to foot up to very high figures; but we bought over 3,000,000 gallons less wine last year than in 1877, and although the import of tobacco was larger, the increase all went into stock, our actual consumption having been less. So also with regard to foreign refined sugar. The bounties paid by France and Holland cannot force us to go on buying augmented quantities which we are unable to pay for, and we accordingly find that the imports of

1878 fell back nearly to the level of 1875—were, in other words, 1,015,000*l*. less in value than in 1877, the last year of our comparative table. In a smaller degree the same is true of silk goods. A process of restriction—natural in our circumstances—has begun, and may be expected to go on. The figures for the current year prove, indeed, that it is going on. In other manufactures of foreign origin this restrictive tendency has not yet, it is true, become very marked, but it may very safely be expected to do so should our poverty increase, unless foreign goods are better and cheaper than those produced at home; should they be so, the fault must lie with our producers, or with the disabilites under which they may lie, and our clear duty is to remove these disabilities should they exist, not to compel the nation to tax itself in order that they may continue to oppress the country. This is the only sound principle on which to proceed as far as we ourselves are concerned.

To revert however to the main point now under discussion, if further proof be required of the absurdity of an attempt to teach foreign nations the blessings of free trade through penal enactments against their manufactures, it will be found in abundance by looking a little more in detail at what a few of them now send us. Our ironmasters declare, for example, that the United States are beating us in our home markets. They must be in a wretchedly weakened state if that be true, for the total value of our imports of iron and steel (wrought or manufactured) from the United States never exceeded 241,000*l*., and was only 200,000*l*. in 1877, while last year it had actually fallen to 177,000*l*. The distress of our tool-makers must be even greater, for they have lately complained with much fervour that American makers are beating Sheffield. They have in fact cried out so bitterly that I turned to the United States official tables, expecting to find there signs of a magnificent and growing export trade in all kinds of cutlery. Great was my astonishment on seeing that for the year ending 30th June, 1878, the total value of the export from the United States to all countries of cutlery, edge-tools, files, and saws together, was only about 200,000*l*. That sum, distributed as it is over all the world, can hardly be said to afford much room for a retaliatory duty here. Nor would there be much room were we to tax every scrap of manufactured iron which the States export, including machinery and steam-engines. It is a trade which is certainly increasing in a small way, but the gross value of it for the year ending 30th June 1878 was only 2,100,000*l*. Of United States cotton and woollen manufactures we get none worth mentioning. I have seen it stated somewhere that 16,000*l*. worth of United States "woollens" were sold in Manchester in 1877, but there is no indication in the United States returns, or our own, that the least progress is being made in the introduction of American woven tissues here. There is consequently no room in this direction for teaching the United States a lesson in free-trade principles. We must find some other way both for fulfilling that charitable object, and, if it must be, for checking the daring competition of the United States cotton cloth weavers in neutral markets. That competition is also a dreadful bugbear to many amongst us, and I am almost afraid to give the figures lest they should haunt our manufacturers in their sleep. Yet the venture must be made, for facts ought never to be blinked, and I have therefore to state boldly that in the year ended 30th June, 1878, the United States exported altogether no less than 126,291,000 yards of cotton goods, value rather less than 2,500,000*l*. sterling. I hope Lancashire will survive that fact, notwithstanding the decrease of its exports from 63,500,000*l*. to about 48,000,000*l*. within four years.[1] If our industrial distress is to

---

[1] A favourite boast of late with writers in the United States has been that they are ousting the English from the Chinese trade. You could not take up any United States newspaper or review of the state of manufactures there without meeting with some snatch of a song of triumph over the great future in store for the manufactures of the

be measured by this terrible competition we must be indeed weak and in need of artificial stimulants.

country in those regions, and I am bound to say that the reading of these had a depressing influence on the mind. There are, however, always two sides to a story, and for the comfort of English manufacturers I give the other version as furnished by the Shanghai correspondent of the *Times* in a letter dated November 14th, 1878. He writes as follows :—

"The discussion in England as to whether the decay of our empire, commercial and otherwise, has not begun, and the confident assertion of the future supremacy of America by an eminent statesman, have caused some amusement here, as well they might. So far as regards China the decay is quite the other way; the position and trade of American firms here seem yearly to decrease, their local carrying trade is extinct, and their import of cotton piece-goods small, unprofitable, and much less significant than certain rhetorical statisticians would have us believe. In order that the commercial position of our country, so far as regards China at least, may be removed from the sphere of argument and lifted into that of fact, I have extracted the following telling figures from the valuable reports on foreign trade for the year 1877 published by the Imperial Maritime Customs. Of the percentages of the imports and exports carried in British and American bottoms the fluctuation of late years has been as follows :—

	Per cent of whole.					
	1872.	1873.	1874.	1875.	1876.	1877.
Great Britain	77·96	76·71	76·30	73·93	71·25	74·39
United States of America	6·45	5·10	4·55	4·54	2·42	1·49

"The share taken by the two nationalities in the coast trade during the same years as represented by the percentage of the values of the goods conveyed under the various foreign flags, is thus shown :—

	Per cent.					
	1872.	1873.	1874.	1875.	1876.	1877.
Great Britain	33·58	37·29	40·25	46·39	40·65	45·72
United States of America	56·81	52·76	45·02	34·49	33·64	5·80

"The decline in the local carrying trade in American bottoms in 1877 as compared with 1876 was caused by the transfer of the steamers of the Shanghai Steam Navigation Company to the Chinese flag. That

The fact of the matter is that the United States have now a smaller export trade in cotton and other manufactures than they had before the Civil War. Their vaunted progress in the export of machinery amounts to no more than this, that the figures of value are now little more than they were fourteen years ago, and as to their exports of raw and manufactured iron, they are now less than they were between 1860 and 1867. How in the world then are we

there are other causes at work is shown by the fact that of the old-established world-famous American hongs in China only one remains. Of the transit trade up country the British percentage had gone from 50·57 per cent in 1876 to 62·11 per cent of the whole in 1877; the American from 25·04 per cent in 1876 to 11·38 per cent in 1877. With regard to the imports of piece-goods into China from Great Britain and America it should be generally known that the total importation was, in 1877, 11,570,000 pieces, valued at Tls.19,000,000, of which 612,000 pieces, valued at Tls.1,600,000, came from the United States. As the whole of the balance came from England, it is idle as yet to speak of competition in this market with America. Experience up to the present time goes to show that, without exception, the efforts made to supplant the English sized light-weight manufactures with pure goods from American mills has resulted in a serious loss to the importers. The present state of the English cotton trade and cotton manufacture is, of course, bad—perhaps about as bad as it possibly can be—but from among the causes which have brought about the present state of things the competition of America in Eastern markets may safely be eliminated. So far at least the problem is simplified."

These statements are exactly what we should expect, and accord fully with the conclusions arrived at in the opening chapter. Much of the export of manufactured goods which United States writers boast about is just forced sales of bankrupts' stock, and nothing else. That also will continue to be the characteristic of it while the present trade policy of the Union is persisted in.

going to punish these people by attacking their manufactures? We may cry out against their selfish determination to close their doors on us, and "do for themselves," as the Scotch phrase it; but we need not add to the folly of weeping the further folly of empty threats.

When we look at the figures of other countries we find the signs of effective competition with our own industries either here or in neutral markets abroad marvellously small considering the disturbance which our merchants and manufacturers are making. Outside her woollen and silk manufactures, already dealt with, France does not send us 1,000,000*l.* worth per annum of any single manufactured article. The highest figure is about 700,000*l.* for cotton manufactures, but that is by no means a steadily growing item, although it was rather larger in 1878 than in 1877. As one would naturally infer also, the same conditions which we find to be generally prevailing in the industries of the leading manufacturing nations are seen in the totals of their exports. They have declined in recent years like our own. The total exports of manufactures from France have been falling off since 1875, when they reached a total of 89,000,000*l.* For last year (1878) the returns give a total of only 75,000,000*l.* These figures do not indicate that France is beating us in the markets of the world. Neither are the Germans beating us in any sense. We ourselves import from Germany no manufactured articles—except refined sugar and woollen yarn—to the extent of anything like 500,000*l.* a year. Of cotton manufactures we have never taken more than 226,000*l.* worth, and now take considerably less. And as to the total export trade of that mushroom empire, what do we find? According to the last figures available in the new number of the *Statistical Abstract for the Principal and other Foreign Countries* (a valuable annual which has been greatly improved by Mr. Giffen), there is very little indication that Germany is seriously competing with us in a manufacturing sense. Her exports of cotton manufactures are utterly insignificant—worth only 665,000*l.* altogether in 1877, or 246,000*l.* less than in 1875. Her exports of pig-iron were worth only 1,740,000*l.* and of machinery only 1,000,000*l.* Even in woollen yarns, certain makes of which Germany is supposed to produce in perfection, the trade is a dwindling one, and was worth only 6,900,000*l.* in 1877, which was less by 2,700,000*l.* than in 1875. Yet Germany, as we have seen, had all through that period protective duties on every one of her manufactures, except pig-iron, and the duty on that was removed only about three years ago. It appears, however, that she has not been protected enough—no country with a dragging and forced trade ever is, if the reckless speculative manufacturers are to be believed—and so Prince Bismarck has come to the help of the poor distressed industries by bestowing on the empire a tariff that is not unlikely to complete their ruin. But though forced through by the domineering energy of the German Chancellor, aided as it always is by his expert and altogether unscrupulous parliamentary tactics, this new drag on German industries has not been unopposed. A strong section of the mercantile community in the country has protested against it without avail, and in the leading ports it has been thoroughly unpopular. Even in the case of the iron industries its probable disastrous effects have not gone unrecognised by manufacturers. They will suffer for the benefit of the producer of the raw material. But on the whole the new law will do good, although not in the direction that Prince Bismarck calculates. The misery it will cause to the poorer sections of the population by its restrictions, not only on a free interchange of manufactures, but likewise on free imports of food, is likely to breed that discontent with the *régime* of grinding, mock-divine imperialism, which may result in the formation of a true and enlightened reform party.

In the meantime, our protectionists and perfervid retaliators might do worse than note the already visible effects of Bismarck's policy on surrounding nations. He is a true retaliator, and carries the doctrine out so consistently that his new tariff imposes discriminating duties on goods coming from countries with high tariffs or with shipping laws considered inimical to German interests. An additional 50 per cent of duty is to be levied on the goods of such countries at discretion of the supreme authorities. Here, therefore, we have reciprocity in full bloom, and if there is any pity under Heaven for the weavers of gaudy cobwebs shot with pretty fancies, the immediate effect of this policy ought to be a general humiliation and repentance on the part of all Germany's neighbours. They are to taste the sweet influences of the lash, and ought forthwith to show signs of reverence to "true free-trade principles." That is the outcome which our truculent "free-traders" tell us to expect; but alas for them! human affairs seem once more in the world's history likely to refuse to be so bound down by finespun brain cobwebs. Instead of humbly submitting to Bismarck, the surrounding nations laugh him to scorn, and seem determined to return blow for blow. "German industries shall be self-sustaining and independent," says the Prince, and he hurls his tariff at the heads of all foreigners. "Be it so," reply those more immediately concerned, "we also shall be independent. You cannot shut us out more effectually than we you. Indeed, Germany is a miserably poor country, whose products are of so little use to us that she may just as well keep them at home, and in future it shall be our endeavour to see that she does so." In this spirit, France, Austria, and Russia, are not merely bent upon doing without German goods, but likewise upon depriving Germany of the large transit trade which her railways now enjoy. A result of this kind is what every one, except dreamers of dreams and persons of natural or assumed stupidity, would expect.

The volume of the present trade of Germany is to some extent obscured by the fact that much of it passes through Holland, and some of the new duties do not come into force till the new year; but we shall not then have long to wait for the visible effects of the tariff. A tariff comprising nearly 275 different duties, ranging from a straw-hat to a sucking-pig, cannot but disorganise German commerce. Even as matters stand, how great is the contrast between Germany and Holland. Our total imports of all kinds from that little country show a remarkably steady increase over the last half-dozen years, and amounted to 20,000,000*l.* in 1877, as compared with 13,300,000*l.* in 1873. But reciprocitarians had better not run away with these figures as helping them in their outcry, for the increase is due to two causes, not altogether pleasant for them to contemplate. One is our growing dependence on foreign food supplies, and the other the extreme lightness of the Dutch import tariff. As to the first, more than one-third of our total imports from Holland may be set down to food products alone. Holland sends us every year, for instance, about 2,000,000*l.* worth of butter, and nearly 1,000,000*l.* worth of cheese. And as to the second—well, what have the reciprocitarians got to say to it? We enjoy, with Holland, a greater degree of reciprocity than with any other Continental country, and we find her trade with us fully more expansive than that of any other country. True our exports thither have been lower of recent years than they were five or six years ago, but the falling off is not serious, and we find that her low import tariff enables her to sell us more. Her exports of manufactures keep up, and her exports of food grow larger. What can our reciprocitarians say to this? Will the imposition of duties on our side mend matters, do they imagine? If the greater the freedom of trade the greater the danger of competition from Holland, how is the restriction of freedom here likely to improve our competitive power against her? Remember we live by our foreign trade; without it we should starve; and whatever weakens our power to maintain it brings starvation nearer our doors. Shall we say that the example of Holland, which admits many of our goods free, and most at a duty of from 3 to 5 per cent *ad valorem*, encourages the belief that competitive force is increased by retaliation? It will be best I fancy to leave the reciprocitarians to answer these questions, and they had better not do it too hurriedly.

This line of inquiry might be pursued to great lengths, but surely enough has been said. If facts have any meaning they distinctly prove that the salvation of the distressed English manufacturer does not lie in the way of retaliatory duties on foreign manufactures. There is no room for their application for one thing, and for another their effect would be to hit hardest just those one or two nations which have advanced farthest on the road towards free trade —that goal which our Platonic free-trader professes to desire that all nations should reach by the application of his reciprocity scourge. Benighted communities like Russia, Spain, or the United States, would laugh at our attempt at revenge, on this line in any case, and Holland, Belgium, and France might also crow over us, for they could steal a march on us with ease if we took to their fetters.

Let reciprocitarians also consider this one other question. How would they propose to deal with the "Most Favoured Nations" Clause, used in nearly all our commercial treaties? Could they insist upon its retention if customs duties were re-imposed here? or have they ever considered what a leverage we have in that clause alone when we come to deal with reluctant foreign protectionists? By being free-traders in greater degree than any other people we can now insist upon the insertion of this clause almost everywhere; but could we do so if we were to try punishment of other nations instead of example? Let the behaviour of Spain on her last revision of her tariff be the answer to that question. Spain has a grievance against this country about her wine duties, and a very just grievance too, and in "revenge" for the non-redress of that grievance she has excluded us from the most favoured position, with the result that the French manufacturer amongst others has a great advantage over us in trading with her. Would not that prove to be a common mode of treating us were we ever to step down from our secure position and higgle over halfpence in the arena of petty national jealousies and childish national spites? Most assuredly it would, and therefore I say there is no room for retaliation in our commercial policy towards foreign manufacturers. Germany, for example, could—and probably would—at once impose her "extra 50. per cent" were we to try issues with her on this ground. A practical illustration of the value of these "Favoured Nation" Clauses was given the other week by the lapse of the treaty between France and Austria. Under that treaty we enjoyed a lower scale of import duties in France than under the Cobden treaty, and now that we have to fall back on the Cobden tariff there is bitter outcry. What should we do were there no more "Favoured Nation" Clauses for us in the future? Community of interests between us and other nations would be abolished for one thing, and our trade would degenerate into mere Ishmaelism. This was very clearly brought out by Mr. Forster in his Bradford speech last spring. Reciprocity means for us tariff wars and nothing else, whereas if we stick to our free trade, and allow other nations to taste the bitterness of their folly to the full, as France and the United States are now doing, and as Germany means to do, we shall triumph in the end.

And even supposing the policy could be adopted, it has now surely been demonstrated that the field over which we could exercise our talents at retaliation against daring foreign manufacturers is a very limited one, and that the countries which that retaliation would affect are quite as few as the varieties of articles which could be taxed.

In regard to raw materials the same conclusion must be come to, although partly on different grounds. Were we to tax raw cotton, flax, hemp, or wool, we might perhaps put some of our colonies, Germany, France, and the United States, to considerable temporary inconvenience, but a few years of that retaliatory policy would see us denuded of our manufacturing industries. To these industries nothing is more essential than cheap production, and to have cheap production we must have absolutely untaxed raw materials. That at least we now have, and it would be suicidal to deprive ourselves of that advantage for the sake of an impotent desire for revenge. Surely this conclusion is self-evident. The stupidest person can see that if we are to sell cheaply, we must buy cheaply, and that a tax of say $\frac{1}{4}d.$ per lb. on cotton, or $2d.$ on wool, would be a clog on the productive powers of the nation, just because by at least so much our powers of selling as cheaply as other nations would be taken away. If notwithstanding such taxes we still competed, it would be at the expense of the working classes, who are already reduced to the greatest straits by the diminution which has been of necessity made in their wages, and by the hardness of the struggle for existence which our forms of social life entail upon them. Workmen coaxed to give ear to the protectionist piping of their masters had better ponder that consideration. The tune is not one they can dance to with safety. We may therefore decide, I hope, that there is no refuge in retaliation as applied to raw materials any more than as applied to manufactures.

CHAPTER III.

SOME MINOR LESSONS OF THE PRESENT TRADE DEPRESSION.

WE are now in a manner half way through the discussion raised in these pages. It may therefore be appropriate to pause here, and try to deduce the lessons which the conclusions thus far reached appear clearly to enforce. There lie still before us the discussion of the reciprocity of bi-metallists, and the yet more important subject of our domestic clogs on industry, involving the question of land-law reform and the capacity of this country to bear taxes on imported food. But in the meantime, the lessons specially applicable to manufacturers and artizans, and fairly deducible from what has been said, may be appropriately enforced.

We can now, in short, proceed to estimate the value of the reciprocity cry and its motives, so far as the trading and industrial classes are concerned, and to point out to them their true policy. The reciprocity wail appears, I think, in the light of the facts to be nothing else than an exhibition of trades-unionism amongst employers and traders. The profits of the master manufacturer have been of late reduced, and he wants to combine with his fellow capitalists for the purpose of forcing the nation to restore those profits by artificial means. That is the spirit of trades-unionism in its basest possible form, and it is a spirit which every intelligent citizen should oppose with all his might. The spirit of the masters is indeed far worse than that of the men when we come to analyse it, and I never see the latter reviled and blamed for their rapacity by the self-righteous opponents of trades-unionism without a certain amount of scorn. The ordinary trades-unionist may be selfish and often ignorant, but neither in selfishness nor ignorance does he reach the standard of his master, who would not scruple to fine the whole nation, if so be that he might in this way make a "profit;" who is so ignorant that he would for the sake of a passing benefit gladly abandon the future to his rivals. We have heard lectures without number regarding the blindness and rapacity of the working man. Will the same rigid moralists now address a few words of admonition to the man's master? I doubt it much. The master wraps up his selfishness in fine phrases about "reciprocity," or in truculent John Bull bluster about retaliation, and the ruck of those who hound down the labouring classes will probably often be found eager encouragers of those blusterers who would bring the whole nation into subjection to their interests. The combination of the few against the many is, it would seem, a good and proper thing; but no curses can be too loud for the masses of work people who try that other combination of the many against the few. To the capitalist, in short, all things are both lawful and expedient; but to the workman and the people the only course open is submission. This doctrine will not, I fear, hold water long, but there may be very bitter struggles to go through before conflicting interests as between capitalists and the people get adjusted. Workmen, too, are every day growing in intelligence and appreciation of the position they hold, and if not misled by the miserable cry of protection, reciprocity, or retaliation, will in turn assert themselves in a fashion likely to disturb the faith of the capitalist not a little. He sets such a good example of fine thorough-going self-seeking, that I confess pity for his case is not the deepest feeling excited. This new phase of trades-unionism amongst masters is at all events likely to alienate from them the sympathy of all thinking minds.[1] Outsiders feel as

[1] Mr. W. E. Forster summed up at Bradford the reciprocity argument in the following terse sentences:—"The argument for reciprocity

the employers of labour themselves must feel, that nothing good can come of this reciprocity cry, whether it be got up to apply taxes on foreign manufactured goods or on raw materials. It is not a cry with any meaning in it at all as an economic remedy for the present stagnation, nor can it be of the least use as a means to induce other nations to adopt free trade. We should not consider that man an object of admiration for his wisdom who chopped off his own right hand in order to teach a neighbour anatomy ; but he would not show greater folly than the people who cry up reciprocity as a palliative for trade distress, or as a sovereign tutor of free trade to other nations. When brought face to face with the facts, we at once see that we are dealing with a barefaced imposition, a fevered dream of minds warped by selfishness and fear; that the men who have taken up this cry are men blinded by a kind of despair, and whom ignorance or passion drives to clutch at the wildest absurdities for relief. Reasoning is probably as much lost on such people as a Latin sermon would be on a Hottentot ; but because they are blind or stupid in their selfishness, it by no means follows that they may

---

is this: You rob the consumer. You are thieves, and persistent thieves. Therefore we shall follow your example and rob your consumers." And he says with great force that were a doctrine like this to prevail the cause of free trade all the world over would be lost.

not temporarily lead the ignorant masses of the nation astray.

Nor must we, because reciprocity is an absurdity as applied to manufactured goods imported by England, be blind to the fact that foreign competition on neutral ground does grow considerably, and foreign self-dependence a very great deal. There is no disputing these facts. Only one or two nations are in any way formidable as yet outside their own borders, but nearly all are seeking by every means in their power to obtain a trade-independence of this country. These facts are extremely depressing, too, especially as we see at present little hope of a speedy return towards free-trade principles in any quarter. Trades-unionism rules abroad as well as here, and the population of other countries, never having known by experience what free trade really implies, or the wonders it works, are still safe in the hands of the dominating manufacturing interests everywhere. Cunning men manage to imbue the popular mind with the notion that the interests of the nation lie in the direction of filling the pockets of a select few, and the patient stupidity of the popular mind gets quite heated with a patriotic desire to uphold at the nation's expense Mr. So-and-So's ironworks, and this or that cotton-mill, as something glorious to the country. One is amazed at the depths of human gullibility visible on all hands, but in nothing is it more manifest than in the clinging to "protection," visible even in such countries as the United States. A recent writer in *Macmillan's Magazine* expressed himself sanguine that the Western farmers of the States would soon cause the policy of the Union to become free-trading. I think he was in that over-sanguine. The farmers will do nothing of the kind till they have found out that protection prevents them from exporting their produce at a profit, and it will depend greatly on the harvests of Europe, and, so far as we are concerned, on our treatment of our own farming interests, whether they find that out soon or late. As long as they are not pushed for money they will be supine.

"Oh, then," the protectionist reader may say, "you admit that it would be a legitimate thing to tax foreign corn, say, or foreign beef and mutton?" I do nothing of the kind. There are other ways of convincing the foreign farmer of the folly of protection than by taxing his corn. That might perhaps bring him to his senses, but as it would bring us meanwhile to misery, there would be little profit in it. On this part of my subject, however, I shall have more to say in succeeding chapters.

For the present it will be well to confine the attention to the palliatives which it may be in our power to apply to the existing state of our manufacturing industries. I say "palliatives" because the radical cure of the evils from which the country now suffers cannot be brought about without much suffering and perhaps a complete revolution in the habits and social laws of the people. There are, however, certain palliatives of the most homely and simple kind which might go a certain way towards mitigating that ultimate contraction of our foreign trade which must, I fear, be considered inevitable, unless the radical changes I speak of do in time come about. In the first place I would recommend our manufacturers to try a little honesty for a change. As a class they have not of late years been distinguished for that quality. The English manufacturer has gone from bad to worse in the adulteration of his cotton and woollen goods, just as the French have done with their silk, until our name has become seriously discredited in all our principal foreign markets. Naturally our rivals in these markets make the most of our defects and probably exaggerate them; but they exist, and, if they are not cured, they will do more to ruin our manufacturing trade than all the prohibitory tariffs that foreign jealousy could devise. In the long run, quality commands the market. If the buyer can be sure of the excellence of an article he will, in nine cases out of ten, higgle little over its price. But, as Mr. Carlyle said years ago in his *Shooting Niagara: and After?* it is just on this one point of quality that English manufacturers, not of tissues merely, but of all kinds, now fail most uniformly. We have acquired the fatal art of " putting a gloss " upon our productions, of turning out things that look well but wear badly; and this art is displayed in everything, from a steam-engine to a pocket-knife. There are still many firms in the country too proud of their good name to make bad steam-engines, and build ships warranted to sink in the first gale. Our Spitalfields silk-weavers still make the finest and most durable fabrics in the world, and there are weavers of broadcloth, as well as of other woollen fabrics, and likewise spinners and weavers of cotton, whose productions no country in the world can equal, whose honourable business repute is above suspicion. All this and more is true, and should gladly be acknowledged; and yet when all is said, the general tone of English business men, and the general quality of English manufactures, have sunk of late years with alarming rapidity. The one aim of the bulk of our merchants and traders has been to make and to sell goods at any price, utterly regardless of honesty or anything else. A race for wealth of the most immoral description has gone on for years, and, becoming keener and more desperate every year, has at length led men to fling behind them everything in the shape of moral rectitude. The very idea of such a quality has been almost forgotten by many, and our "smart" adulterators of goods, our "scamping" manufacturers and dishonest traders, are elevated into a kind of heroes because they have "made money." Epochs in our mercantile history are dated from the occurrence of some huge credit collapse, or from the bursting of some gigantic fraud, the perpetrators of which usually escape all punishment, and even win considerable admiration; they were the unlucky ones where all played the same game. Our trade is thus pervaded with deceit, and has grown rotten and unhealthy in all departments, and unless a better spirit comes over us it must decay and die, coddle it how we may. The more it is coddled, in fact, the more will its rottenness hasten dissolution. Therefore it is that one sovereign remedy for the present depression, and against the disastrous effects of foreign and colonial competition, is a return to the simple sturdy honesty of our fathers. If we cannot so return, the sooner we give place to more honest men the better. The collapses of banking and mercantile credit which we have recently had to mourn over, have lifted a corner of the veil and revealed what is going on beneath. Banking credit and honesty stand or fall together, and the people who can engage in systematic deceptions or frauds for a series of years in the matter of banking, are not likely to be scrupulous about the quality of the goods they make or sell.

Honesty, however, is not all that we require to help us to overcome the troubles by which we are beset; there must be a return to hard work as well. The French mill-hands work as a rule 72 hours a week against our $56\frac{1}{2}$, and this is a discrepancy which no advantages enjoyed by us in the shape of better machinery or higher skill can bridge over. Practically we have in many, perhaps in most cases, no large advantages of this kind. In cotton and woollen weaving or spinning, the probabilities are that we have now almost none. Some very interesting particulars on this point were lately collected by delegates from British Chambers of Commerce who went to France to report on French industries in view of a prospective adverse revision of the French tariff. The reports of these gentlemen cover a variety of our leading manufactures, and the consensus of testimony is to the effect that the industry, thrift, and perseverance of the French workpeople are rapidly enabling them to make goods as cheaply as we can, or cheaper. In regard to Bradford woollen goods, for example, Messrs. Godwin and Ilingworth, the delegates, make out that French mills can be erected for less money than English, that land costs at least as little, and that though machinery and fuel may still be dearer, the mode of working is much more economical. Less fuel is consumed, and a greater use is made of the abundant water-power. And in the matter of wages the advantage is nearly always on the side of France. In some cases we pay as much as 200*l*. for every 100*l*. paid in France, and from 140*l*. to 160*l*. per 100*l*. is a common enough difference. This, too, while the French work 15½ hours per week more than our mill-hands do. Much the same testimony is given by Mr. Joseph Wrigley, of Huddersfield, and Mr. C. E. Bousfield, of Leeds. The average wages paid in those towns is, they say, 25 per cent higher than in France, and the French are little, if at all, behind in their machinery, most of which they now make for themselves. It has been commonly assumed that the English mill-hands are capable of doing more work than the French or any foreign hands, but this seems to be by no means proved. On the contrary, apart from heavy work, such as that of the navvy, or from work requiring great force and energy of body and mind, there is no reason to suppose that the French are behind ourselves. A slightly greater number of workpeople are employed in French woollen-mills than in English, but the delegates say that they "are not disposed to make as much of this point as the French, for this increase in the hands gives the advantage of closer inspection of work, and greater freedom from damage."[1] In the matter of managers, overlookers, dyers, and foremen, the French are said to have the advantage of us. Those at the head of their mills are better educated and of more cultivated taste than the generality of English managers and designers. They are so because in France the State provides better for the primary and technical education of the people than we have hitherto done in this country.

These facts all point a serious moral for the workpeople of England. We have strayed into extravagance on all hands, shortening unduly the hours of labour, increasing wages, increasing the consumption of drink, and have trusted to traditional superiority, or to a fetish belief in the mysterious power of free trade *per se*, rather than to diligence, perseverance, and thrift to maintain our position at the head of the manufacturers of the world. Without copying the better industrial habits of our rivals we could, to say the least of it, do nothing to revive our trade by imitating their confessedly bad fiscal policy.

Try the increased industry and economy first at all

[1] *Commercial Papers*, No. 18 (1878), p. 80.

events. France has gained by these more than ever she did by protection, nay, in spite of protection. The gains she has secured already, where not obtained by hard work, may indeed be all ascribed to the feeble and uncertain steps which she has already taken in the direction of Free Trade. In the Blue Book already quoted, we get some remarkably striking testimony upon this very point. Mr. Frederick Brittain, of Sheffield, in reporting upon the state of the iron and hardware industries of France, has gathered together a great deal of most important information, which I can only in the briefest way allude to. Amongst other things, he states that English ironworkers earn as a rule about 20 per cent more money for nine hours' work than French workmen get for eleven, twelve, or even thirteen hours per day, and that in a large number of cases the difference is as much as 50 per cent. But his most remarkable testimony has reference to the wonderful effects of the Anglo-French commercial treaty of 1860. Previous to that date the French ironmasters had no incentive to exertion. Protected by duties in some cases as high as 130 per cent, they worked lazily on in their old-fashioned ways, recouping themselves for bad work and wasteful methods by exorbitant prices. Thus it happened that the French railways were equipped for the most part by English iron. But since 1860 all this has been changed. Keener competition roused the French to adopt improved methods of manufacture, and so to extend their production that they soon required no foreign aid to enable them to supply their domestic demand for manufactures. They even developed foreign competition; and no wonder, when we consider the meaning of such a history as the following :—

"During the epoch of commercial activity which followed the Franco-German war, the manufacturers and the working men in England and France pursued two opposite systems. In England the colliery proprietors took advantage of the opportunity to raise their prices prodigiously; the ironmasters followed, and a general very heavy augmentation took place in the prices of articles made of iron. At the same time the workmen were able to obtain increased wages, in order to maintain which they manifested a desire to restrict production by diminishing the hours of work. The steel-melters of Sheffield refused to work more than two rounds on Saturday, and the consequence was deplorable waste. While coke cost 40s. per ton, the manufacturers saw their half-used crucibles thrown upon the rubbish heap, although the third round would not have cost half so much time, or half so much fuel, to produce as the first. Sheffield goods were urgently required for every market in the world, and it would have been difficult, by dint of the greatest industry, to supply the abnormal demand; but, unfortunately, English artizans declined to reap the golden harvest, and lost an opportunity that may never return. The conduct of the French was entirely different. Although the prices of coal and iron were affected by what took place in England, the augmentation was not relatively great; and while some of the English workmen were seeking to keep down production, the French were toiling with redoubled energy, and gaining an entrance into markets where they will be henceforward our redoubtable competitors" (*Report*, p. 99).

Could anything show more vividly the terrible dangers to which the conduct of our English workmen has subjected the country? Or is there any conceivable folly greater than that which would cap this extravagance and sloth by the imposition of those very duties whose partial removal has been so beneficial to France? The question needs no answer. These facts are a sermon on thrift and sobriety, which no sensible man can fail to lay to heart. They speak to masters and men alike. The former must restrain their lavish extravagances, in which they have been fatally imitated by their men, and the men must make up their minds to work harder and drink less, and to take lower wages than they have been accustomed to do in the years of fatness now passed away. As Mr. Forster justly observed at Bradford, the well-to-do "Jeshuruns" have waxed fat and kicked quite as much as the poor ones. It has been like master like man, and more energy must be thrown into work on all sides. The young generation of our manufacturers has accustomed itself to a slothful, luxurious—I might even say a diseasedly civilised—life which must, if persisted in, lead it to destruction.

This topic might be enlarged upon to an indefinite extent. Other countries have in other directions advantages which we have let slip. Wages and cost of capital are in our favour as against the United States, but their machinery has been in some respects improved to points far beyond our own. The world has gone on while we have slothfully sat still in our arrogance and pride of wealth, and there must now come repentance, humility, and mended ways. The cry for reciprocity is the cry of those who refuse to see the real facts of the situation. Let them consider this one other point mentioned by Mr. Brittain, that the revenue from our excise and customs rose 9,000,000*l.* in seven years, and say whether they do not think that mending our ways in the matter of drink alone might help us to increase our competing power abroad. Here also master and man have played wanton together in the merry career now rapidly coming to an end.

The chief economic lesson of all such facts as these about wages and long hours of work, or such as those about United States superiority in labour-saving machinery, is, however, this—that nothing can be more hopeless as a means of stimulating prosperity in trade than restrictions of any kind upon producing power. Taxes upon foreign manufactures would not help us in any case, and taxes upon raw materials would merely throw an increased strain upon our labouring poor, just as they throw increased strain on the French or Belgians. Whatever raises the fixed cost of production throws additional burden on labour. This applies with equal force to the mistaken ideas which prevail among workpeople about the limitation of production. Their cry has been "Work less, and prices will rise to paying point." There could be no greater fallacy. Reduction in the hours of labour, and in the resulting out-turn of work, at once makes the profit-earning power of capital less, and does not necessarily raise prices. Prices might possibly be raised did this reduction become universal among all nations, but even that is doubtful, for higher prices at once reduce consumption, and in the end the restrictive policy is beaten by the economy of the consumer. A striking instance of this is seen in the combination entered into last year by the coal-owning railway companies of the United States. These agreed to restrict out-put so as to make higher profits by bigger prices. In the result the combination was a complete failure. Prices did not rise as expected, the only result being that less coal was consumed. The largest of these companies, a company overweighted by inordinate issues of capital, had accordingly to confess a deficit on the year's operations of 2,672,182 dollars, after paying the interest on its bonds, and was driven to the expedient of paying the arrears of its servants' wages in paper, redeemable five months after date. Accordingly the "coal roads" have now adopted the opposite course of unlimited competition. That will no doubt cause great waste of capital for a time, because the coal industry in the States is a huge bubble at best, but when the weakest concerns are ruined, the trade will become healthier.

The true cause of such "over-production" as now distresses artizans and labourers in the United States as well as in England, is inflation of consumption through abuse of credit. Much of the progress so-called, about which we have been so accustomed to boast, has not, in other words, been fair legitimate progress at all. It has been an eager passionate effort to, as it were, forestall and overreach the future. There has been accordingly lavish waste of capital in promoting both the production and consumption of articles beyond natural or prudent requirements. For this waste, capital must ultimately suffer more than labour, and the true way to throw the burden upon capital is not to restrict the amount of labour, but to increase it, for by increasing labour the quantity of product exchangeable at a cheap rate is increased, and that increase is, except in very exceptional circumstances, fatal to concerns which exist exclusively on credit.

The error of the working classes regarding the effective recuperative power of restriction upon out-put or manufacture arises in part from ignorance of the actual position of capital in relation to trade profits. Capital is an excellent servant, but a most imperious master, and the immediate effect of a limitation of production is to make the imperious claims of capital, and, above all, of borrowed capital, instantly paramount. Take the case of a cotton-mill, with a mortgage debt of say 30,000*l.* at 5 per cent. The owners of this mill have to find 1,500*l.* a year to pay that interest, and they may have to find in addition rents and taxes amounting to say 1,500*l.* more before they can earn a penny towards the return of legitimate interest on their own capital, which we might put at say 10,000*l.* Assuming that maintenance of machinery and minor fixed charges are fully another 3,000*l.*, we have a total fixed charge of 6,000*l.* which the mill must earn if it is to pay its way at all, and without making any return on the owner's own capital. Now, if the price of the goods made at this mill is very low, the obvious inference is that, for one thing, the cost of production must be reduced if the mill is to pay. But restriction in manufacture does not tend to reduce this cost. It may reduce the amount paid away as wages, although it can only do that within a sharply-defined subsistence limit; but all other charges for maintenance of works and interest press with increasing heaviness on the owners of the mill. If they sell goods up to only one half the capacity of the mill, and get a slightly higher price for them, their position will still be worse than if they sell up to full capacity at a lower figure. And even if production at a given rate is carried on at a dead loss, the only means of restoring the balance consists in lowering the earnings of the hands, and increasing the amount of work turned out. Stopping the mill altogether involves the complete loss of the capital invested; and every reduction of output, even if accompanied by lower wages, brings the owners nearer and nearer the point of total loss. The results would of course be the same in a case where no debt existed. The owners would lose by restricting production, although the loss would not ruin them so suddenly as if they were loaded with debt.

In short, nothing is more clearly taught by the example we have given, and by all sound economic precepts, than this truth—that incessant and increased labour, and ever-increasing economy of production, will alone suffice to enable the nation to come out of the present industrial struggle victorious. And there is but one mode by which production can be lessened, if that is a necessity. The works and institutions which are unable either from disadvantage in position, or from dead weight of fixed charges, to carry on the struggle to the point of victory, must give place altogether. This weeding process is now going on, and a most painful process it is; but the fact that mills, collieries, and iron-works have been compelled on all hands to stop is only a testimony against the inflation of credit, not a ground for generally restricting production. Those who can stand must do so by working more, not less. Industry and thrift are the true means for conquering foreign tariffs and foreign competition, not retaliatory tariffs, whose effect would be to increase the burdens of the community, and to fetter still more industries already overburdened by fixed charges and by the effects of a disastrous extension of credit. In short, there must be a migration of industry, not a partial cessation of work, along the whole line if wages are to be raised.

We may, indeed, be said to suffer at the present time much more from the effects of over-consumption than from over-production. There has been an excessive consumption of capital for one thing, as well as an excessive diversion of it into channels where it could yield no sure return. As a result, labourers and capitalists alike suffer from the excess of burdens laid upon them, and they must both either work harder or succumb. No royal road out of the difficulty is possible. I say this without prejudice to the hours-of-labour question. It may be that very long hours of labour do not pay in the end, that men who work twelve hours a day wear out sooner than those who work only nine. In some kinds of employment that is probably the case, in others not. But true as that may be, it is also true that we have grown idler of late years. Relaxation has been pushed to an extreme, and luxury and extravagance have grown with the thirst for leisure.

But while thus seeking to enforce the lesson of industry and thrift upon masters and men, while warning the latter that industries which cannot support 100,000 men working to their full capacity, can by no possible device be made to sustain 200,000 working only to half that capacity, it is but fair to admit that there may be general causes at work whose tendency is to make the situation of the working classes of the country one of serious hardship, apart altogether from the troubles besetting particular industries. That there are such causes no one can deny who has taken the trouble to trace with any closeness the actual circumstances in which our working classes are compelled to live. I have insisted on the fact that the working classes of France live on less wages than our own, and, within limits, that is a fair enough ground upon which to urge a reduction of wages here. But it must not be forgotten that the subsistence point is probably much higher in this country than in France. Head for head we are not apparently so heavily taxed as the French, but the incidence of taxation is in this country fully heavier on the poor than it is in France, and our food is very much dearer. I am strongly disposed to agree with Mr. Cliffe Leslie [1] in the opinion that taxes in this country, even when nominally paid by the wealthy classes, really often fall with crushing weight on those below them. No question is probably more difficult to settle than the question of the incidences of local rates, of income- and property-tax, or of stamps and succession duties, and I shall not attempt to settle it here. What little I have to say upon it will, moreover, be more appropriately said when we come to deal with the land laws. But besides this class of taxes, there is the much simpler class of indirect imposts upon articles of consumption, wine, spirits, beer, tea

---

[1] See his Essay on the *Incidence of Imperial and Local Taxation on the Working Classes.*

and tobacco, and that these press far more heavily upon the poor than upon the rich does not admit of a doubt. It is usually said that the poor have the remedy in this case much in their own hands, but that is only partially true. They might, no doubt, restrict their use of articles of consumption bearing customs and excise duties, and so pay less taxes, but the ultimate result of such restriction is a falling off in the demand for our manufactures on the part of those countries which supply most of the articles thus taxed. That falling off must in its turn cause further distress, and so in reality we are driven round to the conclusion that these fiscal burdens ought, in the interests of the country at large, to be reduced or removed. That further step in the direction of free trade is the true course to take, in order to relieve our oppressed industries, and in order to increase the adversity bearing capacity of our working men. The imperial taxation of this country in its present form is, from this point of view, in great need of a reform directly contrary in spirit and intention to that advocated by our protectionists. Our local taxation is even worse, and no one can contemplate the steady increase in the burdens of the lower classes for poor-rates alone without very serious misgivings for the future. When to this is added the steadily growing charges on account of local debt, the prospect becomes more than alarming. Of the burden imposed by this rapid growth of mortgages on the future, the working classes bear more than their full share.

Consider, for example, what the mere subsistence difficulties of our working classes are in the large towns. In the single matter of a roof over their heads, they are driven almost to despair. At the very best, they have probably, as a rule, to live far from their work for the simple reason that there are either no suitable houses near it, or because competition, and the mania for "improvements" have raised rents far beyond their ability to pay. It is hence no uncommon thing for artizans in a large town to have miles of travelling to do every working day of their lives, and that travelling usually costs money, which must be taken as addition to rent. The penny railway ticket which an artizan obtains from the suburban railways lines of London, and by means of which he often travels from one side of the vast city to the other in the early morning and late at night, costs him 6d. a week or 1l. 6s. per annum. So with Liverpool, Glasgow, Manchester, or Birmingham, the frequent omnibus ride is an addition to rent. The fatigue also, and the shortness of the time for rest, must all be taken into account; men, having ofttimes to get up at 4 o'clock in the morning six days in the week in order to be at their work in time. This also involves either poor and insufficient feeding, or additional expense for coffee-house meals, all of which go to impair the capacity of the workmen to endure adversity. Of course this last difficulty hardly applies to factory hands, to colliers, or to the employés of great iron works, but it reaches a vast number of the ordinary artizans and workers at miscellaneous industries throughout the country. And all clogs put on by our taxation, by unfair incidence of taxation, by increased burdens for local improvements, by augmented house-rents and dearer food, apply with much the same force to every poor man throughout the land. Therefore, I think, that some national reform is needed to supplement personal endeavours. We must economise as a nation, and by curtailing the national expenditure for public purposes, acquire the ability to remit more taxes. In short, it is essential to our existence that further progress be made in the direction of complete free trade.

If this conclusion be admitted, and surely it is a rational one, the nervousness of the reciprocitarians at the prospect of augmented foreign tariffs must seem unreasonable. These increased tariffs can only hurt us for a brief period, and in all competition in neutral markets they will not injure us in any shape. On the contrary, they must help us in a very material way, by augmenting the difficulties with which our foreign competitors will have to contend. They will be an increased tax on home consumption, and ultimately on home production, wherever imposed, and must therefore tend to reduce the capacity of the Americans, French (supposing they increase their customs duties), Germans, and others to struggle against us.

The French, however, appear to be beginning to realise something of this since the lapse of the Austro-French Commercial Treaty; and it would not be surprising if a short experience of the higher tariff now in force in France had a wonderful converting influence on French manufacturers and their people. Quite apart from the free-trade convictions and proclivities of several members of the French Cabinet, there are influences at work through the present state of the tariff that may soon bring the French nearer to free trade than they have ever yet been, although for the present the reactionaries may triumph. So also with Germany. Prince Bismarck's folly may end in an irresistible free-trade agitation throughout the Empire, if we will only keep quiet and work hard for a little time. Our direct trade with such countries may doubtless be temporarily further reduced while their protectionist tariffs continue in force; but if we are not seduced into a foolish imitation of their short-sighted policy; if, instead, we are stimulated to increased exertions, increased economies, and further removals of burdens on industry—our own home markets, our Colonial and Indian markets, and, in short, every neutral ground will fall more exclusively into our own hands. We shall therefore do well to forbear from folly, and meanwhile to put our shoulder to the wheel.

CHAPTER IV.

THE GOSPEL OF BI-METALLISM.

BEFORE passing on to discuss the question of our dependence on foreign supplies of food, and the effects of our system of land tenure upon the trading capacity and staying power of the nation, it is well that we should dispose of another section of the reciprocity party. They are known as the "bi-metallists." The leaders of this party, or at all events the most prominent men in it are, in this country, Mr. Ernest Seyd, Mr. Langley, and Mr. Williamson, of Liverpool, but the most assiduous expositor of the theory is, without doubt, Mr. Seyd. He is a man of profound knowledge on the subject, and from his position as an eminent bullion broker in the city and a careful trade statistician, has opportunities of gathering facts together which are enjoyed by few. Chiefly, therefore, from his numerous pamphlets, and from Mr. Williamson's article published in the *Contemporary Review* for April last I have gathered that conception of the theory which I shall now lay before the reader.

Ignoring all the chatter about tariffs and the effects of this or that element favourable to competition against England, enjoyed by other nations, Mr. Seyd and those who think with him lay the whole blame of the present trade depression on the error of England in blindly adhering to "single standard" money. Their theory on this point is in short the same as that of many French economists; and the latest French expounder of it, M. Henri Cernuschi, has probably done more to re-unite the ranks of bi-metallists in this country by his earnest advocacy of "the cause" than even Mr. Seyd. Briefly put, their position is as follows:—

All economists are in error who talk of monetary standards, inasmuch as there can be no arbitrary distinction drawn between gold and silver as media of exchange. Both from time immemorial have been used by the world as money, *i.e.* as the commodity universally exchangeable into other commodities. Both metals thus play a most important part in the commerce of the world, and that nation commits a grievous mistake which ignores the one metal through a sentimental preference for the other, which erects one into an arbitrary "standard" of value to the exclusion of the other. England, the bi-metallists say, made that mistake in 1816 by erecting gold into an exclusive standard of value and condemning silver to a subsidiary position, but she was saved for nearly sixty years from the consequences of her folly by, as Mr. Williamson phrases it, a "practical equilibrium maintained by other countries." All the East, including our own possessions in India, the German agglomeration of states, Austria, Russia, and latterly the Latin monetary union, either used silver in preference to gold, or used both indifferently, with the result that the natural (or artificial) balance of values was not disturbed. Silver-using India and China always absorbed the excess supplies of Europe and America, and England was never, therefore, incommoded by the inability of her debtors to pay her save in silver, because she was always able to exchange their silver for gold at the recognised equivalent value when necessity demanded it. If the East did not want it, the states of the Latin monetary union perforce took it, and by this means the ratio of value between the two metals was kept steady all through the period of greatest gold production without strain or trouble. Such was the position down to 1873, when the gold coinage project of Prince Bismarck began to upset the balance, and since that date, owing to the foolish German imitation of England's policy, everything has gone wrong. Silver has fallen in value, not so much owing to the large amount which Germany has sold, for altogether her sales have been comparatively insignificant, but because of the scare which the demonetisation project caused; still more because of the narrowed market for silver which followed the carrying out of this project. The balance which had practically subsisted since 1816 was, in short, overthrown, and so great was the effect of this overthrow, that it completely demoralised our own Eastern trade, practically dissolved the Latin monetary union, by causing it, and France in particular as the leading member of it, to suspend the free coinage of silver, and threw all silver using countries into a kind of semi-insolvency.

Having demonstrated by this line of reasoning and to their own satisfaction the causes of the present discredited position of silver, it becomes, of course, the easiest thing in the world to indicate the remedy. In one word it is to "restore the balance." If Germany's secession from the silver users has upset the artificial equilibrium, England's accession to the bi-metallic ranks would at once restore it, or at most, the accession of England and the United States. Therefore the bi-metallists urge the institution of a kind of bullionists' propaganda for the rehabilitation of silver as legal tender money in this country; and so enamoured are they of their theory that they predict an outburst of prosperity and splendour for England and for the world such as it never saw before, if only we consent to take the discredited metal into our pockets at a fixed equivalent value with gold. New life will be infused into the commerce of India, the excessive drafts of the Indian council will no longer trouble Eastern merchants; banks trading in that region will no more hang over the bottomless gulf of bankruptcy, trembling lest one more puff of adversity should send them whirling into the abyss. The picture is most attractive and cannot fail to heat the chilled imaginations of traders so familiar all these years with the wintry winds of adversity.

This fairly, though briefly, stated, is the skeleton of the theory of the bi-metallist. Logically it is not at all a weak theory either, if you grant their premises, which I do not. I admit that there is much incoherent nonsense in the customary talk about gold standards and silver standards of value. In a purely artificial sense it is competent for any nation to erect one or other, or both, of these metals into "standards" for itself at fixed ratios of value, but when men proceed to argue as if these artificial creations were products of nature they appear to me to commit a great blunder.

On this point the facts are, I think, dead against the contentions of the bi-metallists. If there be a varying and natural value for the precious metals, determined by the extent of demand for them by popular fancy and by the cost of production, it must be fully more unwise to fix the value of *both* by law than to fix the value of one. In other words, if the "standard of value" superstition be given up, the equivalent values theory on which the bi-metallists base their argument for legislative action in England cannot be sustained. It rests on a pure assumption, to wit, that the customary relation of silver to gold has for a long period of time been as $15\frac{1}{2}$ to 1. The further back you go in the history of the precious metals the less tenable will this assumption prove to be; and ordinary common sense must enable any one to see, that if left to themselves the precious metals would almost constantly vary in their value relations with each other. And they do actually so vary, as it stands to reason that they must. On this point, however, I shall not enlarge. Those who desire to follow it up will find the proof in figures appended to the valuable report of the committee of the House of Commons on silver, which sat in 1876, and also in a more condensed and instructive form in a recent number of Petermann's *Mittheilungen* which contains a monograph written by Dr. Soetbeer on the production of the precious metals since the discovery of America. The figures he gives are of necessity to a considerable extent guesses, but the general knowledge which he has of the facts attending the enormous production of silver in Spanish America, and later of the equally enormous production of gold in Australia and California, is enough to convince any one that the relative value of gold and silver must vary, and vary too from causes apart from the consumption of them. Hence when the bi-metallists say, "You must legalise in England the value of silver in relation to gold which obtained before the late disturbances began," they are making a demand entirely contrary to the spirit of their argument. To be logical on this point they ought to demand the abolition of all legislative enactments in regard to silver or gold, and allow complete free trade to obtain in the metals. They cannot cure the evil of a single standard by adopting a double one, but logically by the abolition of all standards.

An admission that much of the current talk about standards of value may be incoherent nonsense, does not therefore in my view help the bi-metallist arguments. In the practical affairs of life it may be wise on the part of nations to erect such standards single or double, but they must be recognised as purely artificial, and therefore liable to be upset, as they are now utterly upset in France, by changes in the relative value of the metals.

My admission that the other leading argument of

the bi-metallic party is "logical" amounts to even less than what I thus admit on the "standards" controversy. The theory as to the terrible consequences arising from the demonetisation of silver in Germany is based on entirely false premises, and the "perfect chain of reasoning," by which I have been told it is sustained, consequently goes for very little. In its narrowness of view it reminds me of nothing so much as the dictum of the proverbial tanner, whose opinion that there was "nothing like leather" may have been strictly in accordance with his own experience, but yet argued a singularly limited acquaintance with the complex affairs of the world. That bullion dealers or mine owners should fondly imagine gold and silver to be the life-blood of the world, the fountain of weal or woe for all mankind, is probably natural; but it surprises me to find leading men amongst our merchants meekly accepting such opinions as a kind of indisputable authoritative gospel of commercial salvation.

A very summary review of the more conspicuous facts surrounding the silver question, will, I trust, be sufficient to prove that those who go about crying "woe" because Germany has taken to wasting her substance in buying gold are making a great mistake. To begin with, could there, for example, be any more far-fetched or untenable proposition than that urged by Mr. Williamson, in what he calls his diagnosis of the present situation? He says, "The world of late years traded on an effective metallic capital estimated at 1,400,000,000l. Of this we have good evidence for believing that about 750,000,000l. were gold coins and bullion, and 650,000,000l. silver coins and bullion. Now we assert that the world of late has been committing the suicidal act of discarding, discrediting, and cutting off from performing its wonted functions one of the two agents or solvents for the liquidation of balances of international indebtedness;" and further down his essay he asserts that the "hard money capital of the world has been practically reduced from 1,400,000,000l. to 800,000,000l.," all, it would appear, by the action of Germany and the foolish obstinacy of England. Wilder or more unsubstantial ideas it would, I submit, not be possible to put into words. For one thing, it is an almost inconceivable blunder to confound "money" with "capital." It may represent capital, it may be the quickening agent whereby capital is made productive; as the universal medium of exchange it performs a high function in commerce, without which much capital might never be called into being; but that money is not itself capital in any higher sense than corn or potatoes, is proved by the simple fact that the demand for it rises and falls with the rise and fall in the producing capacity of nations. It is even possible to have much money and little floating capital, for that is exactly the position of England at the present moment. The vaults of the Bank of England have been bursting with gold and silver for many months, and yet, judged by the condition of our trade, the capital of the country (its exchangeable wealth) has been steadily diminishing. This new heresy is not Mr. Williamson's alone. The assumption that money—gold and silver, either as coin or bullion—is in some sacred, mysterious, and altogether exceptional way capital, lies at the root of all the reasoning of the bi-metallists, and also informs much of that of their opponents—and a pretty dance the fallacy has led them.

But even were it true that money was in a special sense capital, it would be absurd to assume that the folly of Germany had destroyed half the available "hard money" capital of the world. Gross exaggeration of that kind cannot surely do the bi-metallic propaganda any good. Granting—which is much—that the huge amounts mentioned by Mr. Williamson are in actual existence, they must include the subsidiary internal coinage of all the countries owning metallic money; a large percentage, perhaps two-thirds, of which cannot be considered part of the available international stock in any definite sense whatever.

At the very worst the necessary internal coinage of

the silver-using countries has not been demonetised. The rupee, for example, still circulates in India, and has a functionary power there nearly, if not quite, as great as it had before the Germans began to upset the world's equilibrium. Where its buying power is less, the reduction is due to the smaller supplies of the commodities to be bought, rather than to the shrinkage of the inherent value of the metal. Consequently the sweeping assertion that half the reserve capital of the world has been lost is not merely nonsense, it is an absurdity.

It is time, however, that we should examine the question in its broader aspects, for only in this way can we assign the true causes which have brought about the prolonged trade stagnation from which we still suffer.

In addition to assuming that money—cash—is in a special sense capital, the bi-metallists hold that the isolated action of a single state has done all the mischief. This position is a logical enough deduction from their premises, and it is one held by them in common with many mono-metallists; such, for example, as Mr. Giffen, who, in his paper read before the Statistical Society early in the year, decidedly held that the fall in prices was due to an 'appreciation' of gold brought about by the enlarged consumption of the metal at a time when the supply was diminished. Now I in great measure dissent from this view of the case. It is a view which I think could never be held by men who chose to examine thoroughly the complex elements of our modern credit, modern trade, and modern production. By looking exclusively at the movements of the precious metals, at the amount of them produced, and at the figures—often most inaccurate—of their consumption, writers on money and the functions of money too often come to have an altogether exaggerated conception of what these metals do. Mr. Giffen, for instance, holds that the world has not enough gold, and that therefore prices have fallen; its buying power has increased by reason of its scarcity; yet there was hardly a state bank in Europe which was not, when he wrote, overstocked with the metal. On the same grounds the bi-metallists hold that prices have fallen—measured by the precious metals standard—because one metal has now to do the work formerly done by two. And both these classes of reasoners, strange to say, are familiar with modern banking. They know, as a matter of fact, that by means of the refined adjustments of banking, especially as it prevails in England, and as it increasingly prevails abroad, a bale of cotton or a cental of wheat is as good for purposes of exchange, of buying and selling, as their money or cash equivalent. The business of this country and of the world is at the present day, and through the developments of banking, more completely a business of "barter" than it ever was in the world's history. Commodities buy commodities, and the actual floating capital of a nation is its banking deposits, its productions, and its bills created thereon. From a person with a "balance at his banker's" a cheque—a mere order to pay—is as good a means of liquidating a debt as a bagful of sovereigns. And such an order may be based, not upon a direct right to a store of hard cash at the debtor's credit with the banker, but on bills which represent goods sold. The amount of these bills has been placed at the credit of its customer by the bank, and he draws against that amount. Receipts and payments thus become matters of book-entry, and the floating capital of the world is commensurate with the aggregate amount of its exchangeable commodities.

"But gold and silver are still the universal measure of value for these commodities. Your sack of corn is a pound's worth, or more or less, as the case may be." I do not deny that at all. On the contrary, I say nothing can be truer in fact—only we must not draw a wrong inference from it. I merely wish to point out that the functions of the precious metals are much circumscribed by the modern system of exchange. It is the abundance or otherwise of the thousands of articles exchanged which determines not merely their relative values towards each other, but towards gold or silver. In other words, the functions of these metals are so much circumscribed by modern practices and systems of credit that variations in the supply of the metals cannot have the same direct and marked effect on prices that they may formerly have had. And this being so, those bi-metallists who would correct the troubles of commerce by a partial or complete re-monetisation of silver in England are like nothing so much as a homœopathic doctor who should try to mend a broken leg by doses of arnica globules.

Now it surely follows that if the determining causes of value be much broader to-day than they formerly were, if bank credits and book entries, if cheques and bills of exchange, have increasingly taken the place of hard cash or bank-notes in liquidating debts, the causes of the present industrial distress must also be wider. There must be more in it than either gold or silver can account for. Most assuredly there is—and what the "more" may be is not very difficult to discover. For example, it is just as easy for a time to pay by borrowing as by cash under the modern system ; in fact, far easier. Should I wish to carry on an extensive business, I may either do so by borrowing direct from bankers, or I may create fictitious documents of indebtedness in the shape of bills drawn as if in payment of goods, although no goods exist. By discounting these the means for doing business may be obtained. In a hundred ways, in short, credit can be got by individuals—and as with individuals, so with states and public companies. They can borrow on bonds or shares, and these bonds and shares become just like private bills, media for a further extension of credit. They are called " wealth," and in more or less limited degrees can be made to perform the functions of money or cash.

And what flows from this refined system of borrowing and lending? One thing most assuredly, and that is a far more potent influence upon the prices of commodities than the direct influence of the production or consumption of gold. The borrower obtains money to spend, and in spending creates a demand for commodities, which demand raises their price. Push this description of progress to extreme, carry it on, with but slight breaks, for a generation or so, then behold the fabric thus raised slowly crumbling to pieces before your eyes, and say whether the great wave of depression which is now passing over this country may not have something in it far more important, far more full of warning for the future, than anything that monetary disturbances can mean? We have created a fictitious buying power,—no doubt in the first instance by the aid of the outpour of gold from Australia and California, but going far beyond the scope of that supported by our huge iron production, our enormous manufactures, and above all by the ever-swelling credits based thereon,—and this buying power is now threatening collapse. Nay, it has already largely collapsed, bringing down with it the prices of all goods which it had previously inflated. The "book entries," in short, which have more and more come to represent the wealth of the country, have grown in many instances hollow and unreal; and we not only find the spending and producing capacity of this and other countries curtailed, but "trust"—that confidence which lies at the root of all willingness to take payment in paper for goods purchased—terribly shattered.

How inadequate, then, in the face of a review of facts cited is the explanation that the demonetisation of silver by Germany and the extraordinary demands for gold have ruined the world and lowered prices. Before the mighty effects of "credit and discredit," the "appreciation" or "depreciation" of the precious metals becomes comparatively insignificant.

Still, it may be urged, the action of Germany began the recurrent wave. After all cash—hard money—is the ultimate settler of debts, and therefore it must always be in some definite sense the ruler of credit and prices. That is quite true, but not in the sense usually adopted. Modern banking has so widely extended the effective force of floating capital, and so multiplied its reproductive capacity, that the precious metals usually act rather in a mediate than in an immediate manner upon credit and prices. This is illustrated by the history of our modern commercial panics which did not arise from the actual scarcity or abundance of gold and silver in the banking centres of the world, but from an extension of credit beyond the limits of our producing capacity. We, in one form or other, forestalled and mortgaged our resources to other countries and to each other so rapidly that we came in time to have no means of paying our debts. We could not give "value" in goods for what we had bought, or to cover the promises to pay we had granted. Then our bullion came into play, and had to be parted with, in order to fill the gaps recklessly created. The foundation of credit became shaken, and panic ensued, with its accompanying fall in prices. The movements of gold are thus the barometer of credit; but the gold need not directly control prices. They are ruled by the wise or unwise use of the capital-utilising—or wasting—agencies of modern banking. This kind of control is a very different thing from that usually attributed to gold and silver. The refinements of modern credit, in short, have relegated the precious metals to a comparatively secondary place in the number of agencies utilised for furthering the interchange of commodities between nation and nation, and they only assume the first place when other agencies have been either forestalled or exhausted by reckless speculation and extravagance. Hence it follows that we may have an actual superabundance of the precious metals in our bank coffers, and yet have falling prices, or that in a time of good credit and widespread business confidence, we may have a falling off in the supply and in the actual store of gold accompanying an advance in prices.

I do not of course assert that were the production of gold to be doubled within the next few years, its effect would not be visible in all the money markets of the world, but so to a much greater extent would the effects of five years' overflowing harvests.

It is time now that we should glance at the history of the past thirty years or so from the point of view suggested. In this way it may be possible to arrive at the true conclusion as to the causes of the present industrial disorganisation. It might be too much to hope that by this means the bi-metallic heresy will be finally disposed of; but sensible men, whose minds are not prepossessed, may perhaps be helped to escape contagion.

At what date the troubles from which the commercial world suffers did actually begin it is impossible exactly to state. But we are at all events safe in going back as far as the gold discoveries of Australia and California, or nearly a generation. These discoveries form the most striking landmark, although the true point of departure for an inquiry of this kind is probably the beginning of the railway-building era. The new gold had, however, a most potent influence upon the development of that and cognate modern industries. In the old-fashioned world the gold discoveries would have produced an instant effect in upsetting values everywhere. Prices would have been forced up as the quantity of gold and silver increased, and modern Europe would have been as much impoverished by the influx of precious metal as old Spain was said to have been by the silver and gold of Mexico and Peru.

But the gold came at a most opportune moment to be of great use in aiding an outburst of commercial activity such as the world has never before seen within the same brief space of time. When the great rush to California took place in 1848, England was labouring under a fit of exhaustion consequent on her first wild construction of railways, by which her available capital had become locked up. Men's minds however were filled with new projects for extending these iron roads to the rest of the world, for opening up new mines and new lands, and all that was wanted was the means to develop the wealth which lay in the bowels of the earth. The gold of California, and some three years later that of the British colony of Victoria, furnished this means. It was poured into this country by successful miners, flooding our banks with deposits, affording them a credit-giving capacity never before equalled; it was exchanged for our coal and iron, for our machinery, for railway materials, and for every description of manufacture. India partook in the benefits which this golden rain brought, and, especially after the Mutiny, became a field where immense sums were spent on railways and other public improvements. Through having the start of all other nations in the supply of the great modern needs represented by railways, steam ships, steam machinery and manufacturing gear, England thus utilised for her own purposes and in the first instance the purchasing and credit-making power of most of the new gold. We did not keep the enormous quantities which reached the country idle. On the contrary, as fast as they were received in exchange for our manufactures, coal, &c., from one buyer, they were freely lent at good usury to other buyers, to enable them in turn to pay for more of our goods. A brisk barter on a credit basis was thus kept up, and we grew inordinately rich, both by the profits of trade and by usury. To add to the advantages of our position, and, as it were, clinch our supremacy, other countries got by turns into trouble. First, the United States had their Titanic civil war, the cost of which not only compelled them to part with nearly all the precious metals to foreign countries, but forced them also to contract a huge debt, of which we became large holders. Then Prussia and Austria followed suit, with results disastrous to the latter country—perhaps to both—and the struggle for freedom in Italy in like manner compelled the export of her precious metals and recourse to paper money. So with wars more recent still, they impoverished those engaged in them, and deepened their indebtedness, principally to foreigners.

There has accordingly been a twofold process going on in the world since the modern golden age began, the end in both instances being the same, viz.: to divide mankind into two classes, those of debtor and creditor. As purveyors-general for all nations in the matter of iron roads, tools, and clothes, we have, in the first place, drawn to ourselves the surplus wealth of most of them to an enormous extent; and this wealth we have lent to others, or to the same nations, to enable them either to buy still more of our goods, or to help them to pay for the wars into which they have been drawn or driven. Whether the borrowing was due to the one necessity or to the other, the result has been practically the same—impoverishment for the borrower and enrichment for the lender. We stand to-day—in spite of all our reverses in trade—as the chief tribute-receiving power in the world. All nations pay us, in one shape or other, on account of debts contracted in the strifes or in the progress fever of the generation now passing away. A most abnormal and, I will venture to say, unnatural and temporary state of international relationship has thus been created; and out of this has grown the present "silver difficulty," as well as many others. The rejection of that metal by the spick-and-span new German Empire in her pride, is but one element, though a very serious element, in the case. Silver has depreciated because nations have everywhere got so deeply in debt that they cannot employ even this metal in their ordinary business affairs. If you go into France you will find her flooded with the subsidiary silver coinage of Italy, because Italy is so poor that she has been forced to use paper instead of metal. Paper, for the same reason, has been for the past seventeen years almost the exclusive currency of the United States. Even for small change silver has been nearly altogether disused. So with nearly all the

South American communities. Brazil, the Argentine Confederation, Chili, and Peru—it is paper, paper, on all hands; and now Russia has come in to swell the host of those who cannot help themselves. She certainly has for long been a very sparing user of silver, but not until the recent war with Turkey could it be said to be altogether driven from common use. That war, with its accompanying issues of depreciated inconvertible paper roubles, has completed the disaster which has overtaken silver. So long as it is unused by nations for internal day-to-day transactions, the mere saving of waste materially lessens the consumption. Hence the discredit of silver, in spite of the fact that its supply is not excessive in relation to that of gold, but the reverse;[1] and it is to this state of affairs that the

[1] The following figures, extracted from the annual Circular of Messrs. Wells, Fargo, and Co., the well-known express carriers of the United States, gives the estimated production of gold and silver there in recent years :—

YEAR.	PRODUCTION OF THE UNITED STATES.	
	SILVER.	GOLD.
1870	$17,320,000	$33,750,000
1871	19,286,000	34,398,000
1872	19,924,429	38,177,395
1873	27,483,302	39,206,558
1874	29,699,122	38,466,488
1875	31,635,239	39,968,194
1876	39,292,924	42,886,935
1877	45,846,109	44,880,223
1878	37,248,137	37,576,030

bi-metallist doctrinaires seek to apply the remedy of causing England to decree the "re-monetisation of silver." Argument and illustration are hardly needed to demonstrate the inadequacy of this specific. The causes of the discredit of silver being much more universal than the bi-metallists admit—being, in fact, so altogether different from what they allege, it is obvious that their proposed remedy is a mere nostrum. The whole elaborate theory about a "disturbed balance," which England must restore at all costs, is, in short, and as put by the bi-metallists, a sheer fallacy. The "disturbed balance" is the result of poverty and debt, not of legislative action in this or that country; and to try to cure the effects of inordinate extravagance, of costly wars, of indiscriminate borrowings, by a legislative enactment in regard to silver here, is as absurd as to decree that all men shall henceforth enjoy the same annual income, or that all debts shall from a given date be taken as paid. Were England to decree silver full legal tender for all debts, home and foreign, to-morrow, the mischiefs of the present time might be aggravated, not lessened. A brief reference to the condition of India, and the relations between that empire and ourselves, may help to make this statement more evident. There is, indeed, no stronger instance in support of the views I have

K

here advanced, than that of India. To listen to the bi-metallists, one would suppose that the only thing left for us to do for India in her present poverty would be to take payment of all that she owes us in silver at a fixed valuation. The very fact that they can entertain so preposterous a notion reveals the absurdity of their whole position, and the inadequacy of the causes assigned by them for the present distressed state of our Indian Empire as of most other debt-burdened communities. That the action of Germany precipitated the recent fall in the value of silver is doubtless, in a narrow sense, true; but had that action been all that affected Indian trade, Indian exchanges would long ago have recovered, and Indian trade would not have been so nearly ruined. The one fact that India is now almost precluded from importing silver, except when she borrows to do it, affords sufficient practical demonstration of the truth of this statement. It was indeed clearly enough demonstrated to the Committee of the House of Commons on the Depreciation of Silver, which sat in 1876, that India had become less and less able to import silver in recent years. The causes of this incapacity to absorb the metal are to be found in the rapidity with which debt of all kinds has been piled up by the Indian Government. India's present troubles date, at the very latest, from the time of the Mutiny. The suppression of that outbreak added upwards of 40,000,000*l.* to the funded debt; and her rulers have gone on piling up burdens at great rapidity ever since, until for interest on the funded and floating Government debt alone she has now to pay nearly 6,000,000*l.* a-year, as compared with but about 2,200,000*l.* a quarter of a century ago. Side by side with this debt, her obligations on account of guaranteed railways have also increased; so that her total debt of all descriptions now amounts to fully 237,000,000*l.*, exclusive of the contemplated borrowings of the current year. This involves an annual charge of about 10,500,000*l.* on the revenues of India. Nor is this all. Year after year the so-called Home Charges of the Indian Government for administrative purposes, and for the army, tend to grow; and in this way the balance in favour of India on her foreign trade is more and more completely swallowed up in mere Government and debt charges. The very maintenance of many of the costly public works which we have established in India has, moreover, the effect of swelling the totals on the import side of the trade account, and of still further narrowing the ultimate available balances which can command the import of silver. Those who talk of the amounts which the old East India

Company formerly drew every year from India forget facts like these. That Company did not much trouble itself with the "development" of India, in the modern sense of the term, only with what could be got out of it; and, therefore,—the wants of the natives being few,—the value of the goods imported into the country was comparatively small. For long, also, after that value became large, the constant stream of English capital flowing into India, and the occasional help of high prices obtained here for Indian produce, contributed to hide the end towards which the country was being impelled under the influence of the development craze. But now much of the fictitious aid formerly given to the trade of India has been withdrawn. The Government has to borrow heavily still in this country; but the effects of former extravagance and waste steadily increase the force of the adverse current. Thus the trade of India has become choked by the accumulated obligations of an age of reckless, though, perhaps, in some instances, well-meant exploitation, and of equally reckless resort to the English money-lender.

It is very difficult to obtain an exact account of the various transactions between this country and India over a series of years. The "Statistical Abstract" which should contain complete tables of the home charges, including guaranteed railway interest and surplus profits paid by means of bills or loans, contain no such statement, and an effort to compile them from other sources leads to confusion, so shifting and illusive are most of the Indian accounts furnished to this country. We know, however, that the actual charges of the Government in England have been growing steadily for many years, and now amount to nearly 16,000,000*l.* a year. And it is probable that in addition to these charges there are remittances on private account which bring the total drain borne by the trade of India up to, at a moderate estimate, 18,000,000*l.* a year. Against these figures we have to place the fact that the net balance in favour of India on the foreign trade has not of late years averaged more than 22,700,000*l.* The margin of indebtedness left to be discharged by the remittance of silver has consequently narrowed very materially, and as a natural consequence we find that the average annual import of the precious metals—principally silver—to India has been only about 5,300,000*l.* between 1871 and 1877 inclusive, as compared with an average of 16,300,000*l.* in the previous nine years. In 1878, owing partly to the speculative operations of some of the Indian banks, the import of silver to India was much in excess of the average of recent years; but an exception of that kind only proves the rule.

During the period of greatest activity in railway making, and the period embraced by the "cotton famine," *i.e.* between 1856 and 1867, the imports of treasure in India were never less than 9,500,000*l*. in any one year, and rose twice to upwards of 21,000,000*l*. As the greater portion of these large imports was in silver, it is easy to see how disastrous the effect of a curtailment of the demand, such as took place after 1870, has had on the price of the metal. That it is the cessation of demand from India and from other silver-using countries which has caused the collapse in the prices of silver, and not its excessive supply, is moreover proved by the fact that the fall has not induced increased consumption. Had the absorbing power of debt-laden India, or of debt-laden Russia, Italy, or Brazil been, so to say, normal, a fall in the value of silver, caused solely by German sales, ought to have had the immediate effect of increasing its shipments to these countries in exchange for their produce. That would have presented itself to the speculator's mind as a most profitable transaction, and till these countries became glutted with the metal it would have been so; but no such effect followed, and none such could follow where whole countries lay as it were under mortgage. Practically, as regards India, it is coming to this—that no specie at all can be imported by her, except when her capacity is stimulated by the yearly borrowings of the Viceregal Government in England. The net imports of specie between 1871 and 1878 inclusive have been at the outside 53,000,000*l*., and the amounts borrowed on account of the Government and guaranteed railways in this market have reached in the same time, as near as I can estimate, 23,000,000*l*. To the extent of these loans we may assume that the net import of specie has been increased, and the balance left, which includes 15,000,000*l*. said to have been imported last year, is a mere fraction of the sums which India formerly took.[1]

What is the bearing of these plain figures and perfectly familiar facts upon the bi-metallic question? They demonstrate, I think, with great clearness, that the action of Germany, at all events, has not been the primary cause in the fall of silver. The fall has occurred because silver-using nations have overstretched their resources and are no longer able to buy silver from sheer poverty, and through pressure of debt and other obligations due to foreign creditors. Nor has there been any excessive supply of the metal. Until 1877 the amount of silver imported into the United Kingdom was little in excess of the average,

---

[1] The argument used in this part of the essay is essentially the same as that employed by me in the chapter on the Economic position of India, in my book called the *Resources of Modern Countries*. The prevalence of the bi-metallic fallacy may, I trust, justify its repetition here.

and the 14,000,000*l.* or so imported that year from Germany would have caused but a mere passing flutter in the days of progress by mortgage. And according to a table compiled by Mr. J. Valentine, general superintendent for Messrs. Wells, Fargo, and Co., a well-known authority on this subject, the total production of silver throughout the world between 1849 and 1876 inclusive was only 275,000,000*l.*, of which fully 149,000,000*l.* was sent to India and China. The total production of gold, on the other hand, has amounted over the same period to 643,000,000*l.*, an excess which but for the prodigious waste of wealth which has gone on during the palmy days of the foreign loan traffic, must have materially lowered the value of gold as compared with silver. This merely affords additional proof that those who proclaim bi-metallism as the salvation of mundane affairs are carried away by delusive reasoning. There has, I repeat, been no superabundance of the metal but the reverse, and its depreciation is due to the poverty and extravagance of nations, a cause that no legislative measure can either palliate or remove.

Reverting once more to India, we may, I think, come to this conclusion regarding her present position. Apart altogether from the status of silver as legal-tender money here or anywhere else, India is probably saved from the necessity of exporting her present stock by two things alone. One is the facility with which she is able to borrow in this country, and the other is her opium traffic. This last item in her trade account stands for, on the average, about 11,500,000*l.* per annum. Take that item away and the already imminent insolvency of India would be instant and complete. We could save neither ourselves nor her from a catastrophe such as the world has probably never before seen.

It is, then, to this state of affairs that the bi-metallists propose to apply their silver cure. Their proposal is that England should form a kind of federation with the United States, France, and other countries for the purpose of putting silver on its old footing in relation to gold. Were this done, they assert, the difficulties in regard to the Indian exchanges would at once vanish. The facts I have briefly passed in review contradict that sanguine view. They do more; they prove that the adoption of such a step as this would in a very short space of time destroy the trade of India, and tend to bring those nations in Europe and America still solvent into discredit. The reader will see that this must be so if he considers for a little what the bi-metallist proposals really imply. First of all, they imply a proclamation on the part of England that she will allow all foreign silver-using countries who are in her debt to compound for those debts by paying them in a discredited metal. That is most distinctly the case with regard to India. Were we to make silver "money"—legal tender—at a fixed ratio of value with gold, India would at once ship the metal here in lieu of discredited bills of exchange, in order to liquidate the Government charges. In India the effect of this reversal of the old current of the precious metals towards the East would be in a very short time the substitution of a paper currency for one of silver. She would be denuded of her metallic currency, and through it of much of her available banking capital,—even now, judging by the high rate of interest charged by the Indian banks, far too small. A resort to paper would not only damage the credit of Indian traders, native and foreign, but sooner or later produce a collapse in Indian credit institutions. The Government too, were no remedy applied, must in time find the greatest difficulty in obtaining ways and means to carry on its ordinary business. In proportion as silver became scarce through export, the paper currency would depreciate, and taxes become less productive. Before long it might well be the case, therefore, that the Government of India would lose more by converting paper into silver, in order to pay its way in England, than it now loses on its bills of exchange. Prices would fall likewise— as expressed in silver values—thus causing the exporter of goods to India losses as great as, or greater than, he sustains now.

And what could we do with the metal thus brought home, and taken by us at a value which it now commands in no market of the world? We could not put it into circulation at home, for we have, as a rule, more gold and notes on hand than the internal trade of the country requires. It would only have value if exchangeable into ordinary articles of commerce, and as we already have more currency than we require for that purpose, the only way in which we could utilize it would be by lending it to needy countries, just as we used to lend our great supplies of gold. In order to "revive" business by means of silver we must in short revert to the principle of the pushing tailor who lends his customer five pounds with which to pay for the coat he has supplied. France could not take much of the metal, being already glutted with it to such an extent that the paper currency is circulating on a false standard of value. At the end of last year the amount of silver in the vaults of the Bank of France was 42,300,000*l*., and of gold only 39,400,000*l*., the one metal having steadily increased, while the other has decreased until the gold basis on which the notes of the Bank of France practically circulate is entirely undermined. France therefore would be quite as eager to supply us with silver as India. The United States could not take any of the metal. They also have more on hand than they require, and the only result of a "convention" between us and them for the "re-monetisation" of silver would be that they would increase their shipments of it to London. And where in Europe, Asia, or America, is there another country which would be likely to relieve us of the tons of useless metal thus forced in upon us at a fancy price? I wish the bi-metallists would tell us. They seem to look upon gold and silver as a kind of "fetish" warranted to induce prosperity wherever located, but the facts do not bear out that view. If we make England the receptacle of the available silver now held by nations in her debt, we merely become possessed of so much useless metal, over and above the mass of nearly useless gold usually lying in the vaults of the Bank of England. What we want to bring back prosperity to our manufactures is renewed activity in the exchange of produce, not barter of our goods merely for gold and silver. By merely becoming possessed of the surplus silver of India, we could not insure any increase in the trade of the country with India or with Brazil.

In order to get that increase it would be necessary to lend the metal to India or Brazil again, so that they might pay it away to traders for our manufactures. And that would be the case all round, so much so indeed that without a renewal of the profuse lending of recent years our trade with most silver-using nations would be likely to decrease further under bi-metallism than it has already done because they might strip themselves of what silver they have in preference to selling us goods owing to the greater profit which the sale of the metal to us, at a fancy price, would yield. Their "floating capital," which is often more a matter of "cash," than with us, would therefore be diminished, and their producing power curtailed.

So far, then, as I understand the position, the discredit into which silver has fallen is neither more nor less than the natural result of the extravagance and consequent impoverishment of most of the nations of the world. Through this extravagance and poverty they have become less and less able to employ even the cheaper precious metal in the daily business of life, and this diminished employment has as a matter of course lowered its value. Therefore, the only infallible cure for the depreciation of silver is thrift on the part of the peoples thus poverty-struck—a cure that one cannot hope to see speedily effective. In the case of India, I much fear that it will never be applied at all while Englishmen rule there. Its financial condition grows worse year by year, and no palliative that bi-metallists or any one else could apply will do more than stave off temporarily a catastrophe led up to by generations of wasteful expenditure, and which must shake some day the credit and mercantile supremacy of England to their lowest foundations. We are reaping as we have sown all over the world, and the depreciation of silver is only one prominent symptom among many that a kind of international bankruptcy is hanging over many nations. The weary populations cannot struggle on beneath the burdens heaped upon them by wicked wars, by reckless exploitations of "resources" so-called, or by corrupt and expensive Governments. That is the plain lesson conveyed by cheap silver and mercantile decay, and it is to this much broader and more serious aspect of international affairs that, in my humble opinion, men should address themselves. The inquiry, "How to save nations from impending bankruptcy?" would be a much more valuable one than a narrow and rather foolish propaganda of the wonderfully recuperative force contained in silver. At the very time when the excitement on this subject is drawing to a head, when high Government officials, Bank of England directors, and even Cabinet Ministers, are stated to have become ardent bi-metallists, we are threatened with something which looks very like a depreciation of gold. Had the bi-metallist doctrines been true, had the world been indeed deprived in the way asserted by Mr. Williamson, of nearly half its international circulating medium, the natural consequences would have been a great scarcity of the metal left. It would have been forced into double duties, as it were, and ought to have been most difficult to come by. But nothing of the kind has happened as far as England is concerned. On the contrary, we are still suffering from an excessive supply of that metal. It in a manner weighs on business. We have got it and do not know what to do with it. So much is it in excess of requirements that all our banks and discount houses were but lately longing to see some of it leave us. How is this to be explained on the bi-metallic theory? The "commerce of nations is hopping on one leg," it is said, but what if that leg be more than enough for the wants of the commerce? At present it clearly is so, and while it remains so, a second leg would be a superfluity. We cannot at present buy up cheap silver with our gold, and exchange it for the products of the silver-using countries, because their producing capacity has already been overstrained to exhaustion. They have got to the limits of their tethers for the present, and perhaps beyond them.

Before finally summing up this part of the subject it may be well to advert for one moment to the remarkable influence exerted on "trade balances," as well as the extraordinary part played in upholding and extending credit, by those bonds, &c., which represent the national and corporate debts, of which we have been speaking. I am quite unable to form an estimate of the total debt of the world, but a large part of the corporate obligations of every country of importance, except India and our leading Colonies, is strictly speaking internal debt, and answers in the part played by it in extending credit to the "ready money" of a banker's till. There is beyond this, however, an enormous "international" debt represented by Government obligations of all kinds from consols and French 3 per cents. to Turkish or Peruvian bonds, and according to its market value, and to its transmitability from one centre of business to another, it may be used for the purpose of paying the debt due by one country to another, thus economising the use of gold and silver. In this fashion the heavy trade-balances due by Europe, particularly by England, to the United States, have all hitherto been met. We have surrendered our holdings in United States Government bonds, and in railway or other corporate bonds and shares, to the extent of many millions sterling a year for several years past, in exchange for

American provisions. But for our possession of these bonds we should have had to part with all our surplus gold, and our currency theorists might have been seriously discussing the propriety of adopting an exclusive silver standard to save the country from ruin. By the sale, however, of these bonds the country has been saved from such an infliction. But it has been steadily growing poorer the while, and should the necessity for buying foreign food continue in the same degree, the gold in turn will have to go. Short of consols, the amount of this class of debt-liquidating possession which we may now have cannot well exceed 500,000,000*l*., and an accident to our credit, or to the credit of any state whose people might be probable buyers, could easily reduce it to half that amount. Were India, for instance, to prove unable to meet her debt obligations to us, what foreign country would relieve us of her " securities " ? And were France to have a panic, we might be unable to sell even consols.

Such are some of the considerations suggested by this question of bi-metallism. They show us that the theory on which that nostrum is based is too narrow, that the causes of the present distress are infinitely deeper than any currency tinkering can cure, and that the true source of the existing depression is credit inflation, or, in plain English, excessive debt.

L

To sum the matter up, we have seen that the foolish conduct of the Germans in regard to silver at the most only helped to bring to a head evils of long standing, and when to that was added the exhaustion of India and of other borrowing countries, the elements for a world-wide catastrophe, such as the fall in the value of silver actually is, were complete. We are in the throes of that catastrophe now. Day by day the confusion and deadlock grow greater. Year by year the possibility of emerging from their difficulties without a declaration of bankruptcy has become more hopelessly remote for almost every country under the sun dependent upon silver as its basis of exchange. To such a situation the bi-metallists would apply the homœopathic remedy of a remonetisation of silver in England, in the superstitious belief that mere finance bills drawn in liquidation of obligations which many countries have neither the silver nor the general produce to meet, would be negotiable at an altogether fictitious value. And it is to a situation strained in the manner we have shown that the wiseacres of trade reciprocity would apply the strangely absurd remedy of retaliatory import duties. They would, in other words, restrict the import of foreign goods at the very time when the continued solvency of many countries depends on their power to export goods to a great excess. Were the bi-metallist "remedy" to be applied to the situation, many countries could not even send us silver in payment of their debts, and those who for a time could might soon be ruined by its export. The only hope of such countries, therefore, is to be able to send us more of their general produce. "But we will not have your goods either," the reciprocitarians cry, and so the poor struggling countries must, it seems, be hurled into bankruptcy forthwith in order to save from a like fate imprudent speculators at home.

Surely there ought to be some more excellent way whereby the catastrophe which this state of things threatens might be avoided. Or is it best, I wonder, to hasten the end, to plunge altogether into the vortex of bankruptcy, red revolution, and the demolition of empires? The reciprocitarians seem to think so—if indeed they *can* think at all; but to those not yet led away by their clamours the whole aspect of affairs is too sad and full of distress for the rash application of crude theories. If we are to face our difficulties like men we ought no doubt to do something to restore the value of silver. But to do so we must lighten rather than augment the burdens of the nations that are our debtors, and above all the burdens of India. We must endeavour to draw other nations still solvent into a community of interests with ourselves, so that if possible we may help those that are weak out of the quagmire into which they are rapidly sinking. It may be not possible for us to prevent an international bankruptcy of some kind. The restoration of silver to its old equivalent relations to gold may be, and I believe is, quite beyond anything we can do, but we need not therefore erect further barriers between us and distressed communities. That can only hasten the end and produce universal collapse.

The strain grows more severe everywhere. All international commerce and much of the internal trade of many nations trembles on the edge of an abyss. For some countries no refuge can be said to be left save the free markets of England. Through India the silver difficulty touches us to the quick and makes all our Eastern trade rotten; threatening also, being as it is but the outcome of our extravagance as administrators of that silver country, the stability of our entire Eastern empire. The Turkish war has flooded Russia with paper, depreciating the rouble note by nearly 30 per cent; Austria and Hungary plunge uneasily on under an increasing load of the same unbearable kind; and nearly all South American states still worthy the name draw nearer and nearer to what threatens to be a period of administrative chaos. Shall we turn upon these distressed countries and say, "We will no longer let you sell to us freely; we shall add to your other unbearable burdens the burden of a capricious English import tariff"? To do so would be to involve ourselves to the uttermost in the financial embarrassment and possible bankruptcy now overhanging half the civilised nations of the globe. France, which has always managed its monetary affairs more wisely than ourselves, is at present flooded with the silver of other members of the Latin monetary union, because they in their poverty have been compelled to part with it. The United States have failed to grapple with the silver difficulty. They subsist still upon paper money, and are working steadily towards a new crisis in financial affairs, through the inflation caused by their unreal resumption of specie payments.

The very first effect of the imposition of a reactionary import tariff in this country would probably be the bankruptcy of most South American states, of Russia, Italy, and India. Our imports from these and other countries would instantly shrink, and the recoil of the blow aimed at people whom the ignorant middle-class trade-unionists of this country probably consider their enemies would be ruin at home. Is that what these people want? If so, let them speak out, and we shall know them for what they really are—foolish agitators, intent on hounding the country towards destruction.

It is a remarkable fact, much dwelt on by Mr. Seyd, that the countries most oppressed by the silver difficulty, in common with all those most steeped in debt owed to people outside their own borders, are usually most eager to shelter themselves behind high Customs tariffs. These tariffs are, in fact, at the present moment, to a large extent a sign and measure of their inability to pay twenty shillings in the pound. I am not sure that even France and the United States can be placed in any other category but this. At all events this is the refuge of bankrupt or semi-bankrupt communities, and it is so for a very obvious reason. They all wish to diminish their trade indebtedness abroad in order to be able to meet their foreign debt charges through a larger trade balance in their favour. They think that free trade puts this trade balance too much against them, drains away specie, makes exchange adverse, and leads to bankruptcy. Their panacea therefore has its *raison d'être* to a great extent in the bankruptcy or impending bankruptcy of those who apply it, and they will cling to it till they escape in some way from their perilous situation. This, for example, has been the real cause of the recent folly of Canada, and Canada by her new tariff is hastening the end. Are we to conclude that this country also is in danger of falling into bankruptcy and in need of a crutch to support it? It would seem so; but if it be not so, let us prove that we are still able to help the weak by giving them a free market. Judging by the inventories of our wealth to which deft romancers in figures ever and anon treat us, this country ought to be able to stand anything in the shape of adversity. We are so rich, and take tribute from so many foreign nations, that it seems a cruelty to speak of laying on them additional burdens. Can it be that our wealth is a dream and a delusion? that our fabulous annual income is composed largely of items like the "profits" in the City of Glasgow Bank? that our increased savings are of the kind so admiringly dwelt on by the First Lord of the Admiralty in his great after-dinner speech at the Westminster Palace Hotel? Mr. Smith is a strictly business man, not hitherto suspected of possessing a lively fancy, and yet he gravely told his constituents last spring that during the terrible year 1878 the working classes had actually increased their savings-bank deposits by 1,300,000*l.*, utterly unconscious of the fact that this augmentation was half a million less than the accrued interest at $2\frac{1}{2}$ per cent on the previous year's deposits, or of the fact, nearly as patent, that a large portion of these deposits are not and never have belonged to the so-called "working-class" savings. They are the moneys of the lower middle-class, of young people, and of domestics, and last year many small depositors in ordinary banks transferred their money to the Post-office for greater security. Are we to conclude that all the "tall talk" about our great wealth is mere romancing of this kind—mere increases in debt, and nothing more? It would really seem so, if the reciprocitarians are to be believed. Whatever the real position of this country may be, assuredly it will not be mended by either of the quack specifics under consideration. Both retaliatory tariffs and bi-metallism are remedies of a kind that would convert a slow decline into a "galloping consumption." We may therefore dismiss them from the mind, and try to discover what help is to be found elsewhere.

CHAPTER V.

THE EFFECT OF AMERICAN COMPETITION ON BRITISH AGRICULTURE AND BRITISH LAND LAWS.

WE have now reached the most important division of the subject in hand—the subject of our food supplies and their capacity to bear taxation. Here certainly the taxable area is broad enough, provided the nation can bear the strain which a tax upon food imports would imply. Every year our dependence upon foreign food grains, foreign beef, mutton, and pork, and fresh vegetables and fruit, increases, and the figures are now so large that the longing eyes of reciprocitarians, protectionists, and distressed owners of land are eagerly turned towards them. Here surely relief may be found; here, if anywhere, a cure provided for the dry-rot that is threatening with destruction the old land and the old institutions together.

The total value of our food imports has risen in twenty years time from about 58,000,000*l.* to over

160,000,000*l*. In other words, we imported in 1857 about 18*s*. 3*d*. worth of foreign food per head of the population, and we now import more than 3*l*. worth. It has been no sudden jump either, as the following table relating to a few leading articles of human food will show :—

Articles of Food or Luxury.	Average Consumption Per Head in the Years		
	1857-9.	1865-7.	1875-7.
Cheese . . . . . lb.	1·5	3·6	5·3
Coffee . . . . . ,,	1·3	1·03	0·78
Wheat and wheat flour ,,	78·4	112·6	177·9
Currants, Raisins . ,,	2·4	4·0	4·4
Raw Sugar . . . ,,	31·9	41·5*	62·3*
Spirits . . . galls.	0·17	0·26	0·34
Tea . . . . . . lb.	2·6	3·5	4·5
Tobacco . . . . ,,	1·2	1·3	1·5
Wine . . . . . galls.	0·23	0·43	0·52

* Includes refined, not given in early returns.

Nothing could exceed the eloquence of these figures. They indicate a steady and rapid increase in our dependence on foreign food supplies. The table might be extended, but enough is here given to make plain the extent to which this country is now dependent on others for the means of living. Only ten years ago the value of the consumable articles retained in the country was but 95,000,000*l*. The growth has therefore been much in excess of the increase in population. That has grown only some 17 per cent in the twenty years, but the value of the food imports has grown fully 177 per cent. This table, however, contains exclusively articles of human food or of luxury; but if we go further a field and include such articles as potatoes, rice, barley, oats, and maize, the signs of dependence become if possible still more marked and ominous. Here is a table relating to these :—

Articles.	Average Consumption Per Head in the Years		
	1857-9.	1865-7.	1875-7.
Potatoes . . . lb.	4·3	3·6	21·09
Maize . . . . ,,	23·76	47·04	102·4
Oats . . . . . ,,	16·6	32·1	41·5
Barley . . . . ,,	23·9	27·0	38·1
Rice . . . . . ,,	6·5	3·4	11·5

The "per head" computation is of course in these cases a very rough way of testing the shortness of the home food supply of the people; but it is the only one available, and whether these articles are all used for human food or not makes little matter to the question in hand. The point most worthy of careful attention is the remarkable one that the consumption of necessary articles of food, whether for man or beast, imported to supplement home resources, is increasing at a more rapid rate than the consumption of purely exotic articles. How are we to account for this? The higher prosperity of the nation of late years has enabled it to eat more? Probably so. A very excellent authority, Mr. James Caird, computes that the per-head consumption of wheat, home and foreign, is now over 340 lb. compared with 311 lb. some thirty years ago, and there can at all events be no question that fewer people starve when wheat is cheap than when it is dear. It is however more than doubtful whether this satisfactorily accounts for the enormously-augmented import of some kinds of articles of consumption which has marked our recent foreign trade. There are indications, it seems to me, that our own soil is yielding much less in several respects, and that we have been compelled to supplement our scanty resources to a greater extent on that account. Apart altogether from the question whether we have not had a series of peculiarly unfortunate crops of late, it is surely very striking that such an article as maize, for example, should be so largely used now for feeding horses, and that the import of oats should have considerably more than doubled within twenty years. We can hardly say that cheap food has the same influence in enlarging the consumption of cattle and horses that it has in the case of human beings, and it is a remarkable fact that alongside the growing imports of grains used partly or mainly as food for the lower animals, there has of late years been a decrease in some descriptions of our live-stock. Our stock of cattle in 1876 was $2\frac{1}{2}$ per cent less than in 1875, and $4\frac{1}{2}$ per cent less than in 1874, and that in spite of the fact that a larger area of our soil seems to have been under permanent or artificial grasses. This decrease was probably temporary, as it has since partially disappeared, and in any case it was perhaps to a small extent compensated for by an increase in the number of horses; but, for all that, when coupled with the extraordinary growth of our imports of food, it has an unpleasant significance.

It is of course most difficult to say how much of the decreased yield of our soil may of late have been due to exhaustion, to the poverty of tenants, and the insane waste of natural manures produced by the sewage systems of our towns, or whether it may not in great measure have its origin in the weather. That we have of late had very deficient harvests through bad weather is too well known to need demonstration; but has this cause alone induced the present distress? We must be careful, in dealing with this great question, not to confound temporary and accidental causes with those of a permanent character.

Two or three broad facts stand out with tolerable distinctness in addition to the fact already mentioned that our stock of cattle has been declining. One is the fact that the area under grain crops has been decidedly less during the last six years than during the previous six. Another is that this decrease has by no means been compensated for by an increase in the land under green crops. And yet another is that most of the decrease which is visible under the various forms of tillage is accounted for by a large augmentation in the permanent pasture land of the country. This change has without doubt taken place in deference to the belief—already just giving way before diminished prices for cattle—that this country was destined to be a meat-raising more than a corn-growing country. It is, however, a change that can hardly, I think, have taken place without a diminution in the yield of the soil, else why should an increase in the area devoted to feeding cattle and sheep be accompanied by a decrease in the stock possessed?

Further, the substitution of highly stimulative manures, such as ammonia, guano, and mineral phosphates, for the natural manures now employed in polluting our rivers and in poisoning the people, must have a direct tendency to impoverish the soil. They induce it to yield up its plant-feeding qualities with more rapidity than due regard to recuperation should permit. Thus after a few good crops the soil grows more unkindly, and punishes the cultivator by smaller returns. It becomes, in fact, exhausted.

And again, the course of events during the last few years must have materially lessened the power of the farmers of this country to do justice to the soil. The very mention of artificial manures implies an expensive system of cultivation. In order to keep up the productive powers of the soil constant recourse is had to costly stimulants, which eat in on profits, and when bad years come, on capital. The farmer then becomes less able to meet the wants of the land. He cannot afford to go on galvanizing it into fertility year after year, and a sort of enforced fallow time, to say the best of it, ensues, during which the crops are small, be the season good or bad, and the farmers more familiar with losses and bankruptcy than with profits. The trouble is intensified too by the fact that the tide in prices has turned. Up to 1870 the British farmer can hardly be said to have felt the effects of competition from abroad. The foreign food supply supplemented, but did not overpower, the home supply. And long after 1870 the effects of foreign competition were felt only in grain. Meat continued to rise in price till within the last three or four years, and gave the farmer some compensation. Still, since 1870 the tide has been on the whole against him, and his capacity to meet the exhausting demands of modern scientific systems of cultivation has steadily grown less.

That influences such as these have separately or together been at work upon this country, producing the present distress, is, I think, unquestionable. Our agriculture is languishing to some extent because of our extravagance and folly as displayed in our treatment of the soil. It is the kind of treatment which, continued long enough, would make the entire land nearly barren.

But these are not all the causes of the farmer's present distress. He has had to contend, in addition, with advancing wages. Till very lately the wretched labourer—most forlorn, down-trodden, and hopeless of human beings—was the dumb burden-bearer on whom the farmer could cast the weight of his own disadvantages. If rates, tithes, and rents advanced so as to interfere with the profits otherwise derivable from advancing prices for produce, the farmer could take it out of his slaves, either by employing rather less labour, by paying lower wages, by discontinuing perquisite allowances, or, in conjunction with the landowner, by driving them off the land into pigsty villages or towns, on whose rates they would then become chargeable. The greatest injury ever done by man to man was thus done to the tillers of the soil by those above them. These tillers have for generations been kept as paupers—for the pleasure of "my lord" and "the squire"—until they have sunk to the level of the helots of Sparta—ay, even to the extent, too often, of making them drunk as a moral spectacle to drone homilies over. Their corruptors have cried shame for the good of public morals, and yet have made money fast by selling to them the beer and spirits that wrought their ruin. The beer and spirit retailers swarm over the country by the connivance of, and too often for the profit of, the landowners, and all classes have been degraded by the miserable helotage in which one class has been kept for the profit of the rest. In truth the more beer-shops and gin-palaces there are, the greater the landowner's advantage in two ways. He gets higher rents for his public-houses than for ordinary dwellings, and the consequent larger revenue from excise lessens the necessity for resorting to taxation on real estate for ways and means to carry on the Government.

So the world went well for the landowner and the farmer these many years. Both were making money, and between the two the labouring class was kept degraded in the position of a sot and a slave. But a change has come over the scene at this point also. The serf woke up and demanded the right to live free as other men, strange to say. He saw the men

M

about him, for whom he toiled and sweated his life long, able to spend, thanks to his labour, their thousands and thousands a year. While the squires burst ever into new fields of extravagance, new displays of splendour, the farmer also grew a gentleman—" respectability" was no longer measured by a gig. The landowner's political serf aped his overlord and kept his hunters or his carriage. It was very pretty progress all down the social scale, till the lowest grade was reached; but the effort of the others to push up drove that further down, and the poor hind—the serf's serf—at last cried out. He ventured to say, "This is not fair. Give me the same right to live as you have. I want existence wages *to begin with*." And he struck!

Not much came of his striking directly, but indirectly it has changed many things. What with migration and emigration, wages have been forced up, and the farmer has begun in turn to realise that somehow he is being ground to pieces.[1] Why is it not yet clear to him? So far is it indeed from being clear that he is strongly disposed to take the line adopted by Mr. Chaplin, by certain poor farmers of Essex and others, and boldly to demand protection, a "sliding scale" corn duty, the putting

[1] The following table, extracted from a remarkable article on agricultural depression, published in the *Times* some months ago, will show

THE EFFECT OF AMERICAN COMPETITION.

back of the clock. Whether that would help him or not, we shall see.

In the meantime the considerations here advanced may help, in a general way, to account for the to what extent the action of the labourers of late years has contributed to the financial difficulties of the farmers :—

Year ending Michaelmas.	Nominal weekly wages	Total amount paid.	After deducting 15s. per acre on the grass.*
	s.	£	£ s. d.
1866	12	943	2 0 0
1867	12 and 13	1,034	2 4 11
1868	14	983	2 2 5
1869	12 and 11	982	2 2 4
1870	11 and 12	983	2 2 5
1871	12 and 13	1,065	2 2 6
1872	13, 14, 15	1,298	2 12 10
1873	14	1,230	2 9 8
1874	15	1,263	2 11 4
1875	14 and 15	1,264	2 11 4
1876	14 and 15	1,260	2 11 3
1877	14	1,278	2 12 0
1878	14	1,272	2 11 8

* Average per acre on the arable land.

The average for the thirteen years is 2*l*. 7*s*. 4*d*. an acre on the arable land. The labour bill is more than the rent; and for the last five years has averaged 2*l*. 11*s*. 6*d*., whereas for the six years 1866 to 1871 it was 2*l*. 2*s*. 6*d*. per acre. It will be seen that the increase in the actual cost of labour is out of all proportion to the increase in the nominal rate of wages. This is accounted for partly from the fact that each man does considerably less work for the same money than he formerly did, and partly because the prices of all piece-work now are 30 to 40 per cent higher than they were ten years ago. Besides, the wet seasons of the last few years have occasioned much additional labour, and a great deal of the ordinary work has had to be done over and over again. In 1876, 1877, and 1878, the labour account was to some extent swollen by expenditure in deepening most of the outfall drains of the farm.

remarkable fact that farmers are losing money and unable to compete with those of free countries who own the land they till. If the yield of the soil is falling off, if methods of cultivation are costly or too cumbrous, if prices are falling, or on the average low, and if rents and wages have both been raised of late years, the position of the farmer must have become much that of the grain of wheat between the millstones.

But the reciprocity party, or the "sliding-scale" protectionists, totally ignore all such considerations as these, and rest their case on the alarming extent and power of foreign competition. It is putting down prices, they say, and ruining the agricultural interest in which one-third of the capital of the country is invested. More than that, it is bringing ruin on the nation at large, which has to part with much of its spare capital in order to buy food. Our clear duty is therefore to check the mischief ere it be too late. We must put duties on foreign feeding stuffs—foreign wheat and foreign meat—both to help the farmers and to teach other countries that they had better give up their manufactures and buy ours.

This is the position of Mr. Chaplin, Lord Bateman, and others, who figure prominently before the nation as preachers of the new gospel. I propose to meet that position in due time, but first of all it is necessary to get at the true facts. We must see how far we are being beaten, and by what means. And as the principal hostility of the reciprocitarians in this country is directed towards the United States, it will be best to look at what they are doing, or likely to do. Their competitive power governs that of all other countries, and we must see whether it can also be said to dominate our home production.

The larger half of the foreign supply of such food as we can grow at home now comes from the United States of America. Not only are they able to send us almost unlimited quantities of grain, but throughout the winter season, at all events, they also send us increasing quantities of dead meat. They would send us practically limitless numbers of live cattle but for the Privy Council regulations. We also receive large supplies of corn and of cured and other meats, as well as of the more perishable bulbs and green vegetables, from other countries. It is towards the States, however, that all eyes are directed at the present time. On their capacity for feeding us cheaply we may be said as a manufacturing nation to depend for our very existence, and yet that capacity, as now displayed, is threatening to ruin the British farmer. The late years of distress in the States have led to an unusually rapid extension of the cultivated area. As much as 20 million acres of new soil are estimated to have been brought into cultivation in 1878, and all over the Union there is now a large surplus crop which can be easily exported. We in this country place no restriction whatever on the imports of all kinds of agricultural produce from the States, with the single exception of live cattle. It is felt therefore, and justly felt, to be a most grievous hardship that they should, by the application of a tariff worthy of the dark ages of Spanish tyranny, almost completely shut our goods, in dull times, out of their markets. They refuse to let us "barter" our productions for theirs, and will only take from us hard cash, or the equivalent of such, in the shape of bonds of their debt. Their fiscal policy is thus frankly one-sided and exclusive. It is unhappily also so far as agriculture is concerned successful. In time it may not be so, but at present the disabilities under which the English farmer labours far outweigh the clogs which protection puts upon the free cultivator of the free soil of America. The English farmer may indeed be thankful that his rival is hampered by protection, for without it the battle would be hopeless. As it is the cost of producing food is far greater in England than in America, as an analysis of the facts will show.

In one sense, nothing is perhaps more difficult than the assessment of the cost of production in English agriculture. Conditions of production vary widely over the country, and qualities of soil also vary. But it is possible to strike something like an average, which shall at least give an approximate idea of the cost. Two estimates of the cost of wheat production are before me from different parts of the country, and they may, I think, be taken as a fair average. One is that given in the *Times* of 18th January last, by Mr. Arthur H. Savory, of Addington Manor, Evesham. According to his figures, the net cost of producing one quarter of wheat in the English Midlands is 48s. The other was given me by Mr. James W. Barclay, M.P. for Forfarshire, and applies more particularly to Scotland and the north. According to this, the lowest possible cost at which a quarter of wheat can now be produced is 47s. 6d. In the first estimate, rent, rates, and taxes are taken at 45s. per acre, and in the second, rent alone is placed at 30s., so that reckoning taxes the same throughout, in the one instance more is allowed for labour, manure, &c., than in the other. Substantially, however, these estimates agree in the result, and they may be taken as a fair indication of the total cost of producing a quarter of wheat in ordinary years, the crop in both cases being assumed as four quarters, or thirty-two bushels to the acre, which is above rather than below the average yield in this country of late years.

The cost of producing butcher's meat is fully more difficult to estimate, but I am informed by Mr. Barclay, who has closely investigated the subject, that meat cannot be produced in this country under 67*s.* 6*d.* to 70*s.* per cwt. of dead carcase, or $7\frac{1}{4}d.$ to $7\frac{1}{2}d.$ per lb.

Now let us see how these figures compare with estimates of production in America. The figures for that country are also very scanty. In many parts of the States farming is pursued with little or no regard to economy, and with no attempt at careful tillage. A large proportion also of the new settlers have had no previous experience in farming. Hence the average yield of wheat per acre in the American Union is low when compared with that of this country. Mr. George Osborn, of Kingston, Canada, furnished the *Times* of February 27th, 1879, with some figures upon this point, which I shall here quote :—

"The cost per acre in the spring-wheat States— Iowa, Nebraska, Dakota, Minnesota, and Wisconsin :— Ploughing, $1 50*c.*; dragging and sowing, $1 ; seed, $1 50*c.* ; harvesting, $2 5*c.* — $6 50*c.*; equal to 1*l.* 6*s.* 9*d.*, to which must be added 10*c.*, or 5*d.*

sterling, per bushel for thrashing, &c. For new land add $2, or 8s. 4d. sterling, for breaking. Minnesota certainly raises more wheat to the acre than any other State in the Union, her average for the last 10 years being nearly 16 bushels per acre. Taking the United States as a whole, I find the average for the last five years ending 1877 to be very slightly under 11 bushels per acre. The spring-wheat States named above have on an average for five years produced a fraction over 13 bushels per acre. The greatest known yearly average of Ohio, the largest producer of the winter-wheat States, is $17\frac{1}{2}$ bushels; while the average for 10 years, as officially shown, is 10·55 bushels per acre. Illinois produces year by year not more than 10 bushels per acre; Iowa, 14 bushels; California, 13; Kansas, 13; Wisconsin, 14."

These figures do not in all respects tally with those given for the cost of production in England, but making all allowance for discrepancies, they may be taken as indicating that the fair average cost of producing one quarter of wheat in the American Union does not exceed 20s. That is also the estimate of Mr. Barclay. On good settled land, such as a great deal of the land in most of the States now is, the average yield of wheat is higher, and the average cost of production of course less.[1]

[1] The Earl of Airlie takes exception to this statement in his able and interesting article on "Agricultural Prospects," which appeared in the *Fortnightly Review*, for July, 1879. He says :—"This statement is not borne out by facts. With the single exception of Ohio, which appears

Against this, however, another consideration has to be taken into account in the shape of interest on capital borrowed. In order to exhibit with vividness the actual position of the majority of American farmers, and the conditions under which they work, it will be interesting to place side by side with Mr. Osborn's figures some *data* which I have received from an experienced banker in Chicago. Writing to me under date 31st December, 1878, he says:—

" Within this territory good fertile farms sell at from 20*s*. to 5*l*. per acre, averaging now probably

to possess an extraordinarily rich soil, the average yield of wheat per acre is greater in the more newly settled and less in the older States. Thus Illinois produces barely ten bushels per acre, Iowa fourteen, and Minnesota sixteen. Not only is this the case, but it is an ascertained fact that the yield has fallen off in those States which have been largest settled. It is said that in California the yield has fallen from twenty to thirteen or fourteen bushels. The late President Lincoln told me that in his younger days winter wheat was successfully grown in Illinois, but that then (1864) the land would not stand it, and they were obliged to sow spring wheat." And he proceeds to point out that this is due to the tendency of early settlers to exhaust the soil speedily by taking crop after crop without manure. He admits, however, that its productiveness may be restored by manuring and by deeper cultivation, and these remedies are, I am told, being at the present time much more widely applied than they were a few years ago. In the nature of things it should tend to be so. After the first squatter comes the regular farmer, who settles on the land as owner, and strives to make the most of it. Stocks of cattle also increase, and with their increase comes greater ability to manure the land and to till it thoroughly. The aid of labour-saving machinery is likewise called in wherever possible, and the result is that the fertility of the soil is not merely restored, but maintained. Nor need this restoration and maintenance involve about 5*l.*, and taxes are about 1*s.* 2*d.* per acre. The yield of corn is from twenty to seventy bushels, of sixty pounds. Good farmers will average fifty, and the whole would average about forty bushels per acre, on good corn ground.

"To illustrate, suppose the farmer in debt for full value of his land, hiring all the labour performed, and selling his entire crop without feeding any part of it to stock, and the account would be as follows :—

"Interest one year on 5*l.* 4*s.* 2*d.* at 8 per cent, 8*s.* 4*d.* ; taxes say 1*s.* 2*d.* ; labour of growing and harvesting, 24*s.* ; total 34*s.* 6*d.*, for which he would

---

the great extra cost of cultivation which Lord Airlie says must suffice in time to make the position of the American farmer subject to as great disabilities as farmers here, for where the soil is naturally good, the natural manures, provided by good stock and careful husbandry, should be almost enough to maintain its fertility. They might not altogether do so because the crops are so much exported that the soil must inevitably get in some degree impoverished. As to present facts, I believe Lord Airlie has been misinformed on the features of the case. President Lincoln's statement about Illinois when made may possibly have been correct, but I am assured that it is not so now. There is more winter than spring wheat produced in Illinois, and so far from the fertility of the soil decreasing, it is increasing there and elsewhere. Actual facts, therefore, correspond with what one would suppose to be the case. There can be no doubt that the tendency of agriculture in America is to improve. A first swarm of speculative cultivators may partially exhaust the soil, but as it falls into the hands of steady hard-working proprietors, it will be treated by them with the same loving care that peasant proprietors universally exhibit in Europe. There is therefore no consolation for the British farmer in the statements of Lord Airlie. Cost of production will not tend to rise much in the Union under existing conditions, and were the Union to reduce its protective tariff, it might be so materially lowered as almost to extinguish the rent-paying capacity of much of the soil in this country.

have for each acre of land, forty bushels of corn, costing say 11*d*. per bushel, with ordinarily an average of 1*s*. 6*d*. per bushel at the farm, and now worth about 1*s*. ½*d*. In some places as low possibly as 8*d*., and in others as high as 2*s*."

The figures given in this extract apply to maize or Indian corn, of which very heavy crops are grown in Illinois. They show that the cost of producing that cereal, now imported by us to the extent of nearly 10 million quarters per annum, does not amount to more than 7*s*. 6*d*. per quarter. But the chief value of this information lies in the picture it gives of the condition of the farmers. They pay no rent, their land is seldom heavily mortgaged, they have not got heavy manure or labour bills to pay, they till the lands with their own hands, and their taxation is comparatively light—all circumstances in remarkable contrast to the position of farmers in this country. If the farmers in the wheat-growing States are in the same position as those of Illinois, and there is no reason to suppose that they are not, it is easy to believe that 20*s*. per quarter is by no means an under estimate of the net cost of growing wheat there.

Accepting that figure, we must next add the cost of carriage to England, in order to arrive at the relative positions of English and American farmers in the markets here. In one sense the American farmer is at an immense disadvantage, since he must perforce pay two freights, as it were. His tariff prevents the import of goods to the States, so that the ships which bring corn to England from America often go there empty, or with a few tons of pig-iron taken as ballast at a freight of 1s. per ton. Notwithstanding this disadvantage, which applies in some degree to American railways, as well as to the shipping trade, the freight to this country is almost ludicrously small compared with the charges on our home railways. It does not average probably one-fifth, and in some instances is less than one-tenth, of what farmers in this country pay for moving their crops to market.

According to a list of through freights, kindly supplied to me by a Liverpool merchant, about 9s. 6d. per quarter appears to be the total charge for carriage from Chicago to Liverpool, and rather more than 8s. 6d. per quarter from Detroit to the same port. If therefore we place the entire cost of carriage per quarter of wheat, including terminal charges at both ends, at 10s., we shall be dealing liberally, and that sum added to the estimated cost of production brings the net cost price of American wheat delivered in Liverpool up to just 30s. per quarter. If that wheat is sold at an average of 35s. per quarter, the American farmer and his intermediaries will have a profit of 5s. per quarter to divide between them.

All the farmer's outlay is indeed met by the 20*s*. per quarter. The price of 35*s*., moreover, is fully 12*s*. 6*d*. below the net cost of production in this country. Moderately stated, this therefore is the probable measure of the disadvantage at which the English farmer now stands in competing with the United States. On 3⅜ quarters of wheat, which is the net average yield per acre in this country in good seasons, after allowing for seed, this represents a disadvantage of fully 40*s*. per acre, or more than the average rent which the English farmer now pays. In other words, the American producer is able to sell his wheat in Liverpool at a price which must prove utterly ruinous to our agricultural interests as they now stand.[1]

[1] Here again Lord Airlie enters an objection to my estimate of carriage, because I say nothing about cost of conveyance of grain to Chicago from the inland regions. That cost, he says, is often heavy, and I admit that to a great extent he is right. I question, however, whether the general effect of the calculations given in the text is much weakened by this consideration. Not only is the constant tendency of freights towards greater cheapness in even the outlying districts of the west, as those who have been unwise enough to put money in railways there ruefully know, but throughout a considerable part of the year the estimate given by me is itself an exaggerated one. The magnificent water carriage enjoyed by the States of the lake region helps to make the cost of carriage from outlying districts to Chicago or to the sea exceedingly low during summer. This advantage is increased by the canal and river competition to the ports. Now that the mouth of the Mississippi has been deepened, so as to admit of vessels of large tonnage loading at New Orleans, these advantages of the American farmer in river, lake, and canal navigation will probably be still more conspicuous.

The position of the cattle-farmer in this country is now not much better, and promises to become rapidly worse. Of the cost of rearing cattle in America there is, so far as I am aware, no ready means of judging; but there is no ground for supposing that it is relatively greater than the cost of growing corn. On the contrary, there is good reason for assuming that it is less. Pasture on the State Domains is still so abundant that in many parts of America young animals can be reared for an inappreciable expense. The cost of fattening them for the market is thus compressed into a very short period of time, and involves small outlay. The practical test, however, of the cost is the price at which American beef can be sold in England. Now some recent shipments of American dead meat have been sold in London in excellent condition at $6\frac{1}{2}d.$ per lb., and I am told that had it been sold at $5\frac{1}{2}d.$ it would still have left a profit.

There is no room to doubt the accuracy of that statement, for in the United States fresh dead meat can, I believe, be bought freely at from 4 to 5 cents per lb., or roughly at from $2d.$ to $2\frac{1}{2}d.$ At that price

---

Thus every year will probably see freights in America, and from America to Europe, reduced lower and lower, or, at all events, kept at a level which our capital over-burdened English lines cannot approach without courting a deeper gulf of bankruptcy than that with which most American lines have at one time or other been familiar.

an ordinary carcase would represent a value of from 6*l.* to 8*l.*, which I am told is about the average price of fat cattle in the Western States of the Union. Here again, however, the producer has freight against him, as he must pay not only the double charges necessitated by the one-sided character of the trade, but also an additional sum for rapid transit and for scientifically perfected means of conveyance. My Liverpool friend has kindly given me the current figures on this point also, and they show that the cost of carrying live cattle from Chicago to Liverpool about equals the value of the beasts in Chicago. For dead meat the charges are, I believe, practically the same. It will be well to leave the live animals out of reckoning, as the import of these will probably be much reduced by the effect of the cattle-disease legislation. The figures above given enable us, however, to make a rough estimate of the relative positions of the producers of beef in the Western States of America and in this country. We find that a Western farmer can deliver fresh meat without loss in Liverpool at something under $5\frac{1}{2}d.$ per lb., as against $7\frac{1}{4}d.$, the lowest price endurable by the farmers in this country.

There is plenty of evidence that these estimates cannot be considered exaggerated. We see it in the great increase in the imports of live cattle which took place last year, an increase that stimulated not a little the activity of our legislature in taking measures to guard against disease. Last year 86,600 live cattle were landed at the principal ports of the United Kingdom, or 67,000 more than in the previous year. The imports of dead meat are equally convincing on this point, as the following statement will prove :—

Imports of Dead Meat.	1876.	1877.	1878.
	Cwts.	Cwts.	Cwts.
Bacon	2,810,000	2,395,000	3,467,000
Beef—Salted	243,000	208,000	219,000
,, Fresh [1]	171,000	465,000	504,000
Hams	349,000	424,000	797,000
Pork — Fresh and Salted (not Hams)	377,000	304,000	388,000
Meats — Salted or otherwise preserved	376,000	606,000	584,000
Total	4,326,000	4,402,000	5,959,000

The increase in 1878 on the figures for 1876 is nearly 37½ per cent, a most startling fact in view of the trade depression from which we suffer, and a fact, too, of incalculable significance with reference to English agriculture.

All the evidence available, in short, points to the defeat of the British farmer in the competition. He cannot, weighted as he is, stand up against the comparatively unencumbered Americans. A new world

[1] Chiefly from the United States.

has come into being within less than a generation, and the landowners and landholders of England have not yet begun to recognise what its existence means for them. They accordingly dream of protecting themselves by the imposition of duties on foreign agricultural produce. As monopolists face to face with "free trade" in their own domain, the landowners are disposed to fly to the usual refuge of such, the refuge, to wit, of a protective tariff. They would punish the United States by levying heavy duties on the beef or grain imported thence, permitting only such of our colonies as behaved well in the matter of tariffs to send their produce here duty free or nearly so. And the farmers appear to be only too willing to join their landlords in attaining this object.

Is it a good object? Can it be attained without injury to the community? Let us see once more what the facts say; and be it remembered that in all this discussion we have as much as possible kept out of sight merely temporary causes of loss to the British farmer. His distress is great, and it is a distress which can now be mitigated only, not removed, by "bumper" harvests. For a generation at least forces at home have been at work putting obstacles in his way. Without any adequate hold on the land, he has seen his profits gradually eaten in upon by rent and other augmenting charges. The extravagance of the time has also told upon him; cost of cultivation has increased; and when everything was in a manner working at high pressure, new competitors sprang into the field. They had him at a great disadvantage on the mere ground of tenure alone, and the inflation amid which he lived only aggravated, did not primarily cause, the ruin with which he is now threatened.

To these circumstances the reactionary party would now apply a protective tariff. They boldly say—Tax foreign agricultural produce for the benefit of the English farmer, and—this *sotto voce*—the English landlord. These distressed parties constitute a trades union, in short, and demand that the nation should tax itself for their benefit.

The first and most obvious answer to such a demand is that we *dare not* take any step which would tend to increase the cost of living to the masses of the nation. The course of our history for the last generation and a half has brought us to this terrible dilemma. Our people must be fed cheaply or perish, and the only present means we have of feeding them cheaply is by the purchase of food produced abroad. The nation has altogether outgrown the actual productive capacity of its land. Since the beginning of this century the population of Great Britain has about doubled, and the whole of that increase has crowded into manufacturing cities and towns. The rural population is not only not larger than it was some eighty years ago, but it is absolutely smaller, and tends to decrease. Thus the great masses of the nation have become divorced from the soil. They are cooped up in the towns, and have no means of subsistence but the wages they earn. As towns have grown in size and numbers, the cost of living within them has in many ways risen, rents have advanced, taxes are higher, and locomotion more expensive. I question also if it does not take more to sustain life in full vigour in the large cities under the artificial conditions of existence imposed there. At all events the children born and reared there are less robust than their parents were who came fresh from the country. A "weediness" appears about the young of the great manufacturing towns that promises ill for the future of our race.

But putting that aside, and looking merely at the actual condition of the people of this country, it is apparent that, for weal or woe, we have become a nation of artizans and manufacturers which cannot grow food for itself, and it is absolutely essential to our existence that we should sell what we make. In no other way can we live, and in order to be able to sell we must be able to produce cheaply. The cost of subsistence must therefore be low, because without cheap food low wages and full working vigour could not be maintained together.

Look at the condition of large sections of the working classes during the past winter. Owing to the stagnant position of many industries distress has prevailed—nay, prevails now in nearly every important centre of manufacture—pauperism has increased, relief funds have had to be instituted. Hundreds of thousands of people have been living on the confines of starvation, and yet wheat was cheaper during all that winter than it ever was before at the same period of the year within living memory. Wheat was all last winter and spring from 12*s.* to 15*s.* per quarter lower in price than it was in the winter of 1877-78. Still a majority of the population of the country has barely been able to exist; large numbers cannot exist at all at any time except on charity, and *such* charity! Could they have lived any the more easily had the price of grain been raised several shillings a quarter by the imposition of an import duty? Is there indeed any more grim commentary upon the folly of those who hint at the imposition of such a duty in any form than the condition of large masses of the population at the present time? If that says anything intelligible to the political economist it says that these people are already overburdened—that they want relief from existing taxes, not the imposition of more. If to these other burdens we now add a tax on bread we shall assuredly see riot and bloodshed, perhaps even revolution abroad in the land at no distant day. If we in normal times—thanks to the constitution of our society, to the monopoly of the chief sources of wealth enjoyed by the few, and to our poor law—have one in thirty of our population absolute paupers, how many should we have were bread dear and, as the inevitable consequence, work scarce? Why, at the present moment, thousands upon thousands of the population of this country formerly earning their livings respectably are hovering on the brink of utter destitution. In all our towns, in the manufacturing centres, and in the rural districts of many parts of England, thousands of families have been existing for some considerable time on the proceeds of bills of sale granted on their household goods. The state of such people is growing desperate beyond belief, and yet the selfishness of the protectionists would increase their woes.

"But the farmers are in distress, and our agricultural interests must be preserved and upheld." Certainly, nothing can be more laudable or more necessary; the only question is, How are they to be upheld? Heavy corn duties—or light for that matter—did not sustain the farming class in affluence in past times. On the contrary, agriculture was never in a more wretchedly backward and poverty-stricken condition than when the country enjoyed the blessings of the "sliding-scale" of heavy corn duties.

True, there was not in those times the superabundant foreign supply which now competes with the home production, but neither was there the present large population to feed. To the great bulk of that population cheap food is essential to existence; to all our manufacturers it is as imperatively necessary as cheap raw materials; and even supposing that duties on corn and cattle would help the landowner and farmer for a time to draw large rents and profits from the soil, the ruin they would thus bring upon the nation at large could not be borne. It would soon recoil, too, on the landowners. As a matter of fact, we are dealing here with a monopoly—a monopoly of the very worst kind. At the door of this monopoly, much more than anywhere else, we must lay the bulk of the troubles from which the nation now suffers, and all that threatens to be permanently ruinous in the position of our farmers. The pleadings of men like Mr. Chaplin are the cry of those who possess, and who have for many generations enjoyed, the exclusive benefit of this monopoly, for protection at the nation's expense against forces that their own selfish greed and folly may be said to have in no small degree called into being. The manner in which the soil of this kingdom is held back from the people is one of the darkest features in our social economy and one of the greatest causes of our present distress. No words can adequately depict the dangers with which it threatens us. While the population has been pressing into towns and outgrowing the native means of subsistence to an extent which entails an import of the necessaries of life to the extent of nearly 100 millions sterling a year, and a total import of articles of consumption of more than 160 millions a year, the landowners have done nothing to relieve the pressure. On the contrary, they have often aggravated it. Mr. Caird, in an essay of his lately published, says that "This country is becoming every ten years less and less of a farm and more and more of a meadow, a garden, and a playground."[1] And he goes on to speak of the deer-forests, grouse-moors, pleasure-commons, &c., in a tone of admiration. A more melancholy description we have seldom read. Instead of being a matter for congratulation it is something to lament over with the profoundest sorrow. Enriched by the labours of the multitude, by the opening of railways, by the working of mines whose "royalties" ought never to have been theirs at all, by the extension of towns over lands whose free-

---

[1] *The Landed Interest and the Supply of Food.* By Jas. Caird, C.B. (Cassell, Petter, and Galpin.)

holds are chiefly in their hands, the small group of men who own most of the soil of the kingdom have sought to turn it into a hunting-ground—a garden of pleasure. They have enlarged their vermin-preserves, their deer-parks, their grouse-moors, and fox-hunting districts, and set more store by the life of a rabbit— most destructive of land pests—than on human life. No liberty has been given to the cultivators of the soil to put capital into their farms. Throughout Great Britain the tenant has little or no hold on the land, little or no security for his money. In many places he is but a yearly tenant, liable to be turned off at six months' notice. In short, as Mr. Bear admirably puts it in his article on the " Liberal Party and the Farmers" in the *Fortnightly Review* for March, 1878, "Our whole land system, from beginning to end, is now tending to the impoverishment of landlords, tenants, labourers, and consumers alike, and it is one of the most striking evidences of the indomitable energy and enterprise of the Anglo-Saxon race that British farming has, under such monstrous disadvantages, advanced to even its present state of comparative excellence." It can advance no further. If this wretched land system be not changed, and that speedily, the farmers must fall back into the besotting poverty of the corn duties' times, or perhaps give up cultivation altogether; an alternative which, however serenely it may be contemplated by men of the dry intellectual stamp of Lord Derby, would not, I fear, suit the monopolists of the soil. They could not live by "sport" alone. Already there are signs on all hands that the farmers' capital is becoming exhausted. Their rent alone absorbs it, in many instances, and they are so oppressed between the demands of the landowner and the small return from their crops, that they have ceased to cultivate with energy. Of what use is the charity dole of 10 or 15 per cent deducted from rents as a remedy for the utter hopelessness of defeat which facts like those given above imply? Landlords should not deceive themselves; such petty charities will not stave off the evil day much longer. They will have to assent to many reforms before many years are over,—under penalties. Either the hungry population will give them notice to quit altogether, or it will desert the country in such numbers as to cripple our industrial forces beyond remedy. When the wants of the population are considered, when we look at the urgent food requirements of the masses that fill our towns, or behold the soil untilled or half-tilled, the rural population deserting their homes because they cannot live—500 labourers of Kent, for instance, going in a body to a foreign land—it is enough to make us despair of the future. A flush of sudden wealth has blinded the landowning class, or they surely would long since have seen rocks ahead threatening the ship of the State with destruction. It was Lord Derby, I believe, who some years ago gave currency to the statement that, with proper tillage, the yield of the soil of England could be doubled, and those who know anything of agriculture are not disposed to question the estimate. With our population, the soil ought to be cultivated like a garden. And what would doubling the yield of the soil mean? For one thing it would mean a power to export instead of a necessity to import food. We should be able then to say to the Americans with effect: "Keep your food at home, we can feed ourselves." That surely would be a safer way of obtaining revenge on American exclusiveness than import duties would be. The American farmer deprived of our market would soon find out what "protection" meant at home, and demand freedom to buy where he pleased.

This in few words is the reform most urgently needed in England. The land must be delivered from its bondage and given back to the people. Until the Liberal party is prepared to take up this great question, it will fail to be the party of true progress, and will deserve to continue at the mercy of reactionary administrations, good only for creating difficulties, for misleading the nation, for heaping on the people new burdens, and by their very folly and wrongheadedness, goading the people on to demand what their nominal leaders refuse to give.

It is a gigantic task no doubt, but if the landowning class wishes to escape ejectment by way of revolution, it must give way in time. In no civilised country in the world is there now a class with such exclusive privileges and such preponderating political influence as the small group of landowners, who, in this country, hold the life of the nation in their grasp More than half the soil of the United Kingdom is nominally owned by some 2,000 persons. According to a valuable analysis of the very ill-arranged and incomplete parliamentary return of the landowners of the United Kingdom, published in the *Financial Reform Almanac* for 1878, 421 persons are the owners of 22,880,755 acres, or nearly 5 million acres, more than one-fourth of the total area of the United Kingdom. The mind is unable to grasp what such a monopoly costs the country, but certain features of it stand forth with a prominence sufficiently notable. In a most absolute sense, the well-being of the entire population of some 32 million souls is placed in the power of a few thousands. For these thousands the multitude toils, and it may be on occasion starves. Hence it is that all through rural England we have continually before us that most saddening of all spectacles, two or three families living in great splendour, and hard by their gates the miserably poor, the abject slaves of the soil, whose sole hope in life is too often the workhouse—that famous device against revolution paid for by the middle class—and the pauper's grave.

Our landowners have not merely burdened the land with their game preserves; they have tied it up, and actively conspired to prevent its due cultivation. Instead of rising to the true necessities of the case, they cling to their game, make penal enactments about it, and struggle to augment the intensity of the evil which it is to the people, as if the very existence of the country depended upon hares and rabbits.

In his absolute supremacy the landowner overrides all justice, takes precedence of all ordinary creditors on his helpless tenants' estates, and controls the system of cultivation, often in utter disregard of private rights or private judgment; and in addition secures to himself the absolute reversion of every improvement which the tenant may make on the land. To his exclusive privileges and overmastering claims we owe it that our modern cities are built well-nigh as insecurely as the "paper houses" of Japan, so that three-fourths of modern London may need to be rebuilt within thirty years. Add to these considerations the fact that the landlord contrives to throw on his tenant, and through him on the people at large, the greater part of the burden of local rates and imperial taxation, and we have a few of the more prominent features of the abject slavery of the British people to a few thousands of their number. At the present moment, for example, land is assessed for imperial taxation on the basis of a valuation made in the reign of William and Mary. Apportioned in fixed amounts among the several counties of England, that valuation is practically in force to this day, except where the modified tax has been redeemed. Were a 4s. tax—which was the levy under William and Mary—to be imposed on the present valuation of real property, it would yield a revenue of about 29,000,000l. a year; whereas the existing tax yields little more than 1,000,000l.[1] The landowners avoid paying this tax, but make up for it in part by voting for licences to public-houses on each other's property so as to keep up the income from excise and their own rents, and in part by laying the burden of "rates" as heavily as possible on their tenants.

Surely it is time that all these things should be changed. While the landowners have played at game-preserving the world has gone on. Free peoples

[1] Vide *The Financial Reform Almanac for* 1878 and 1879—a somewhat crotchety, but too little known publication.

have sprung up in regions where English feudalism is unknown, and these peoples are crushing our farmers to the dust. They can feed us at prices that defy competition, and many among us would perish of hunger if they did not send us this food. Of what use is it to erect barriers to keep out the benefits which thus come to us? Would they do aught save hasten our ruin? Alas for the folly that would cling to such rotten driftwood in the storm! The true remedy for many things in England is—*To set the land free!* Let the landlords think of it and submit now, lest it soon be too late. The best remedy for all our industrial distress, the best relief for our overcrowded towns, is to let the people go back to the soil. Free trade in other directions has sealed the doom of feudalism and land-monopoly, and it would be well for the nation and for the landlords themselves if they could realise this now, instead of going about to increase discontent and misery by the application of old-world nostrums—instead of harking back to a fiscal policy which has perished with us I trust for ever. It will at all events be a woful day for the British landowners when protection comes back; for its return is the surest means of goading the crowded and hungry population of our towns to rise up and seize what they will consider their own. God forbid that we should have revolutions here, but they will come in spite of us if this great need of our time be not met—if, instead of it, deluded farmers and blindly selfish owners of the land conspire together to put new burdens on the backs of our already sorely overburdened population.

CHAPTER VI.

RADICAL CURES FOR THE EVILS OF FEUDALISM.

THE remedy for our present distress as well as the prevention of future dangers indicated at the conclusion of the previous chapter is not one that the landowners of this country, as a body, like to contemplate. They dread what may be implied in the words "set the land free," or "free-trade in land," and even the most enlightened among them propose palliations instead of remedies. During last Parliamentary session a Commission was appointed at the instance of Mr. Chaplin, M.P. for Mid-Lincolnshire, for the purpose of inquiring into the state of agriculture in this and other countries; and, judging by the composition of that Commission, I should say that its principal business will be to endeavour to find a justification for the reimposition of import duties on foreign food grains. Much attention is to be devoted to the United States, no less than four deputy Commissioners being sent out to gather information about all sorts of things, useful and of no use, relating to agriculture there; and at home the investigation is likely to be devoted to showing the misery of landlords, rather than to the effect of the land's bondage on the well-being of the community.

Dread of revolution will, I firmly believe, prevent the landowning classes from daring to go the length of reimposing corn duties in any form, but that this Commission will succeed in finding reasons for protecting agriculture there can hardly be a doubt. Yet one is sometimes almost driven to regret that something of the nature of a revolution is not possible for us. When one examines closely the position of the British farmer, and observes the mischievous effects of the existing land system, one is driven almost to despair to find an efficient, and at the same time constitutionally-practicable remedy. The conviction forces itself on the mind, that the only thorough remedy possible is a revolutionary one. I mean, of course, revolution strictly "limited." In other words, the true cure for the existing land-monopoly mischief is one that must be forced on the upper classes by the necessities and miseries of the millions whom their pernicious and altogether unjustifiable usurpation of popular rights has forced into ill-built, over-crowded towns and made dependent on industries whose prosperity can only be maintained by our having the world for a marketplace. Should corn duties be reimposed, a revolutionary upheaval of a more or less threatening character is almost certain, and the landowning class knows this full well. No patent poor-law device for saving the upper classes will prevent trouble among our crowded population if trade be chained and bread made dear. On the contrary, the poor law might in such circumstances well become one of the most powerful incentives to revolutionary action among the lower middle class. Free emigration, that best and surest of all our safety-valves, cannot even be trusted to stave off the evil day, for millions cannot emigrate at once, and if they did the country would only be the more hopelessly involved in the decay and social confusion which cause evil humours to generate. Therefore the reactionary landlords now intent on proving that the country must perish if they be not protected, are beating the air: Did they succeed in their objects, their selfish efforts to save themselves would bring down on their heads such a freeing of the soil as the wildest Irish radical hardly dreams of. A new corn duty would be a notice to quit for every great landowner in the kingdom before it had been two years in operation. It would be their turn then to emigrate after the manner pointed out by Lord Derby as the one alternative left for the distressed, dissatisfied British farmer.

The truth of the matter is that the bondage of the people to the landowners in this country is rapidly becoming intolerable under the limited free trade now enjoyed, and nothing save great and lasting concessions can long save us from internal convulsion of some kind. We have been saved more by accident than good management hitherto; but the multitudes whom we were content to drive out of the country are now sending from their new homes messages of freedom in the shape of cheap food raised on free soil. These messages have a significance that no land-monopolists can disregard. Our landlords may inquire, and discourse, and struggle, but they will have to yield, and the longer they struggle the greater the chance of their ultimate destruction by the fierce hot lava-outburst from below. Is it to be imagined that 10,000 or 100,000 men armed with parchments can stand the shock of 30,000,000 of impoverished people?

Before passing on to discuss what plausible or practicable remedies lie to hand, by means of which the landowning oligarchy which now rules, as for many centuries it has ruled, England, may break their fall or stave off a fate too horrible to contemplate, it will be well to give the reader some idea of the nature of the loads which have in some shape to be removed from the soil. All that I can say here, or that mortal pen could write, would give but a faint image of the thousandfold evils which we groan under in consequence of the existing land monopoly, but a few facts may serve as rushlights to reveal the darkness.

We must first of all revert to the fact that the present concentration of land in few hands is the result of a gross perversion of customs and laws prevalent in this country, more or less, since the earliest dawn of our civilisation. Some of these customs and laws, as any student of the land question well knows, are founded on rights belonging, not to the individual, but to the community, and so to the nation, or to the "crown" as the nation's representative. Gradually, however, by frauds, by persistent assertions of authority, by defiance of the rights of the weaker, and often under a show of legality, the people—the nation—has been deprived of its rights in the soil, and they are all now practically centred in the landowner. He has all the rights, and those under him all the duties, and he has been able to attain to this lofty position because he has been the law-maker. We boast of our parliamentary system, and with reason. The nation owes much to it, in that it has at times when the nation has spoken out done what the people wished. But on the whole, and in relation to the land more particularly, this parliamentary system has been the most costly, the most dishonest, and withal the most corrupt peace-keeper with which any intelligent community was ever burdened. For many a long day Parliament was in no sense an assembly of the people's representatives, but of the representatives of the great nobles and the landowning oligarchy. And after all our reform bills it is so still to a greater extent than its panegyrists would have us believe. Not only is the House of Lords a non-elastic self-representing body, but at least four-fifths of the House of Commons is directly or indirectly controlled by the landed interest. While our present system of choosing representatives is maintained this absurdity is likely to continue. We have indeed paid dearly for the glorious British election, with its accompaniment of candidates paying heavily for the "honour and privilege" of "representing" us in Parliament. No gratuitously-rendered service in this world is in the long run good for much, and gratuitous Parliamentary service is about the worst gift that the English common people ever had. What it has cost them in land robbery alone no one could calculate.

We can, however, tell with some vividness where practically all this fine system has driven the nation in these latter days. The effects of a class monopoly lie bare to the eye in the congestion of our population and the distress of our agriculturists. Lord Derby and others are great on "freedom of contract," and eloquent in deprecating any kind of interference between landlord and tenant, as a breach of the true principles of political economy. This is very pretty language, but it has no actual relevancy to the facts of the case. For to begin with, land is itself something of which in one form or other certain people must have in a sense a monopoly. The monopoly may be modified in its injurious effects by strict laws, by minute subdivision among the people, by the exaction of part of the profits in the shape of land-tax for the benefit of the whole nation, but a monopoly it is, and a monopoly it will remain. When, therefore, the landowners of this country talk grandly about freedom of contract, they talk about a thing which cannot possibly exist in the sense usually understood by the phrase. If one party to the bargain enjoys the exclusive rights involved in a monopoly, it must be obvious that the other party is at an enormous disadvantage, and that is exactly the position as between the British landowner and the unhappy man who lives by tilling the land. For a time the true relations of the two may be hidden, or partially disguised, but it cannot long be so. I have called the farmers of this country "serfs," and I will prove the title correct by examples of the way "freedom of contract" is understood by the landlords.

The chief proof will be found in the agreements or "leases" which the landowning class deign at times in some parts of the country to give to their tenants. Such leases as I have been able to obtain a sight or copy of are Scotch, and may be held inapplicable as illustrations of what prevails in England. But in point of fact the illustration these leases give of the power of the land-monopolist is even more forcible in reference to England than to Scotland. Faint shadows of rights still linger in the latter country, but have mostly long ago disappeared in England. The tenants in Scotland, for example, as a rule have leases of some kind; but in many parts of England the tenants remain on the soil, and are permitted to till it absolutely and entirely at their overlord's will and pleasure. He can turn them off at two years' notice should they displease him, and, by virtue of his exclusive rights as a creditor, seize on everything the poor tenants have in defiance of other creditors, if he so chooses. Quite recently, for example, I read the report of a summing-up by an English judge in a distraint case, which showed that not only can an English landlord levy distress on the goods and chattels on a farm in utter disregard not merely of the tenant's other creditors, but actually of whose the property may be which the bailiffs may find on the land. In this instance distraint was made on sheep belonging to a third party, that had been put on the farm to feed, and this distraint was held to be good in law.[1]

In the matter of game preserving, moreover, the two parts of the kingdom are much on a par. A landlord in both can ruin his tenants if he chooses, up to a point which will leave him safe, come of the tenant's other creditors what may. On the whole perhaps in this case the lease-holder has the worst of it, because his farm may be nearly free of game when he enters upon it, and afterwards be eaten up by the vermin which the landlord fosters and rears at his expense. Still he is disposed to struggle on and hope against hope, while his tenant-at-will compatriot in England may fling up his holding and emigrate if he be a man above serfdom, or grovel along in abject dependence if he be not—the mere tool of his overlord, a slave of the most degraded of all types. The fact that these game laws alone should in any form exist in a civilised country, and above all in a country crowded like ours, is the strongest possible proof that the land-monopolists have made laws only for themselves, and not for the people, and that the state of the British farmer is a state of humiliating bondage. For the sake of

[1] *Vide* Lord-Justice Baggallay's summing-up in the case, Lake *v.* Duppa, printed in pamphlet form, and sold by Effingham Wilson.

"sport," men's lives are sacrificed, men's characters warped, our jails filled, hard-working, honest yeomen and peasants robbed, the land left untilled or but half-tilled, food made dearer, and all to please a few thousands out of this great nation. These laws are a standing disgrace to us, and are alone sufficient to bring on the landowning oligarchy a terrible retribution when the whirligig of time brings its revenges.

But we must now revert to the character of farm leases. The general principle underlying them all is the summary one, that all persons and things upon the land or under the land exist for the sole and exclusive use and benefit of the legal owner or life-renter of the soil. This general principle is illustrated by conditions such as the following, which I select from the "Articles, Regulations, and Conditions" applicable to the letting of land on the Scotch estates of "His Grace the Duke of Richmond and Gordon," president of the new Agricultural Commission, and a man of large territorial possessions both in England and Scotland. As the clauses are lengthy, I am compelled partially to condense them :—

The lease, usually for nineteen years, excludes all but direct heirs, and refuses power to sublet. The whole expense of the documents connected with the lease falls on the lessee. Power is reserved by the proprietor to plant trees where he pleases on the land leased on giving compensation. He may open mines and work them, or search for minerals at pleasure, on paying surface damage only. He can mark out and construct roads at will, taking the materials without compensation, save where arable land is broken up by quarries. Alterations in existing roads or public places can be made by him also at will. The whole of the game of every description is reserved for the landowner, with full power for himself to hunt and shoot over the land, and the tenants are to protect the game as much as in their power from poachers. All fishing in the rivers and streams on the estate is forbidden during the close time fixed by Act of Parliament, under pain of forfeiture of the lease and eviction. This applies to the tenant or to any of his family. All corn which the tenants may want ground must be sent to the Duke's mills on the estate, and they are bound to pay "the accustomed multures, knaveships, mill-dues, and services" charged at these mills. Should drainage work be carried out on the farms, the tenants must always carry the materials without payment, and may, at his Grace's pleasure, be made to pay for the materials as well as to do the work. Should he, however, elect to do the work, the tenant must pay 5 per cent. on the outlay as additional rent.

Under penalty of paying 6*l*. per acre rent for each departure from the routine, the tenants are bound in the customary terms to crop their land on the "five-shift system," *i.e.* are tied hand and foot in their manner of dealing with the soil, and that frequently by men who probably know as much about practical farming as about practical cookery. Minute particulars as to quality and kinds of seed, as to manuring, &c., are specified, and bind the action of the tenant as thoroughly as if he were a convict on the treadmill. The tenant is also forbidden to burn, sell, or remove any of the straw, dung, or turnips produced on the land. All must be used on the spot, or sold to the owner at a valuation, in the event of the tenant leaving the farm. Without apparently having any opportunity for investigation, the man who once signs an agreement for a lease is by that act considered to have agreed to take all fences and farm buildings as being in a state of complete repair, and is bound to uphold them in that condition throughout the term of the lease, to the landlord's satisfaction. All the protection a new tenant has consists in a claim against the outgoing tenant, which the landlord makes over to him to do his best with in the event of the buildings, &c., proving out of repair. The landlord may inspect the buildings, &c., at will, and the tenant is bound to paint the outside woodwork of the houses once in three years at his own expense, as also to insure the buildings and crops at their full value, solely for the landlord's benefit—all such charges being in addition to the rent. A tenant falling in arrears with his rent for one year may be summarily ejected—the law of hypothec, like the law of distress, giving the landlord full power to recoup himself out of the farm stock, and regardless of everybody's interest save his own. Fencing or inclosing can be ordered to be done by the landlord on any part of his land, and the tenant must provide and lay down the stones for such fencing, or in the event of the landlord deciding to plant hedges, must protect these hedges with fences. Half the cost only of the future maintenance of these fences will be borne by the landlord. No cottage or garden on a farm can be let by the farmer without the written consent of the overlord. Heather or moorland grass which protects game must not be burned by tenants or their servants, under penalty of an additional rent of 2*l.* for every fifty acres of holding being levied for the unexpired term of any lease. Written permission may, however, be given at stated periods to burn such heath or moorland in limited quantities.

Such are the leading provisions under which

the Duke of Richmond and Gordon agrees to let his Scotch lands. They accord with those of other proprietors in that country. Some that I have examined are more stringent and humiliating, others less so; but the above will show very well the general tenor of these agreements. We need only mention further that many landlords exact payment in labour in addition to rent, commanding their tenants, for example, to drive fuel for them gratis. Others exact so many fowls or eggs at stated seasons. In England, again, it is a common enough habit on the part of sporting landlords to compel their tenants to rear dogs for sporting purposes—the dogs being of course owned by the landlord, and designed for his exclusive enjoyment.

Now I ask any candid, unprejudiced person who reads this bald summary whether these one-sided stipulations indicate that "freedom to make contracts" for which the landlords of this country always plead when the demand for reform is made? Would such a state of bondage be tolerated by men in any other walk of life? Conceive a shoemaker bound by the man who lets him a shop to buy his leather at a particular tannery, to make only one kind of boots, or to sell only to customers who had boots made to measure, or to supply so many days' labour a year in addition to a money rent. These stipulations would not be one whit more absurd or enterprise-stifling than those contained in ninety-nine out of every hundred of the leases or agreements under which men in this country till the soil. And the reason why these men are compelled to submit is, that they have to deal with a monopoly the most powerful, the most jealously-guarded, and the most exclusive that can possibly exist. The owning of land must confer peculiar privileges on the owners in any event, for land is of limited extent, and the complex arrangements of civilised communities prevent all from being cultivators, even where there might be enough for all. But in no country have the privileges of landowning been so determinedly kept in the hands of a few thousand men as in Great Britain and Ireland. In no country, therefore, have the effects of this monopoly been so disastrous on the life and habits of the community at large. I confess to a heart-sinking amounting almost to despair of the future of this country when I consider but the one fact of the extent to which the working of this landlord power has conjested the population into huge towns. I go into the "slums" of London now and then, and the sights I see fill me with horror. What a herd of hungry pariahs we are rearing there, and in all the large cities of the kingdom. What dreariness fills the life of the toiling millions who are huddled together there, breeding diseases physical and moral. Some day terrible developments may come of the unnatural life lived in these most desolate, though overcrowded regions of great towns, into which much of the best blood of the country has been driven by the operation of English feudal laws and the all-grasping folly of English landowners. But we have not immediately to do with that point. The question before us is, How to deal with this gigantic land monopoly? "Set the land free," we say; but how? It will, I think, be easily comprehended that perfect free trade in land is an unattainable thing. You cannot transfer it like corn, or tea and sugar. There must always be some class in the community which will enjoy some of the benefits of its possession more than others. It is a natural monopoly whose working and effects no amount of legislation, however well conceived, can wholly neutralise.

That being so, it has always struck me that the phrase, "Free-trade in land," is to some degree misleading. In a modified sense alone could it be true at best, and in a country where wealth is concentrated in comparatively few hands it might be most difficult to make it true to any important extent. Hence the remedies most commonly proposed, the plans devised for breaking down the existing pernicious form of the monopoly, are all more or less inadequate. What all land-law reformers want is the return of the population to the tillage and ownership of the soil in much larger numbers than now. We want to put it in the power of the farmer, or the peasant, or the retired tradesman with agricultural tastes—and who is there who does not at times dream that he has such?—to buy land in patches which they could cultivate in perfect security. The magical effects of property in land, of complete security for capital expended, the sense of living on one's own land, and labouring for one's own good undisturbed by vexatious landlords, perfectly free from bondage, in short, would—all experience proves—exercise a most wonderful influence on the productiveness of the soil. For the perfunctory tillage of a slave would be exchanged the loving, watchful husbandry of a freeman, and the change would do more to liberate England from its social and economic troubles than all the cunning tariffs that human ingenuity could frame.

The means proposed, however, for effecting this beneficial change are, as a rule, inadequate, clumsy, and illogical. Most advocates of land-reform confine themselves to urging the abolition of the law of primogeniture and the prohibition of the custom of entail, coupling therewith a simple and cheap system of registry for land transfers. These proposed

P

changes are most excellent as far as they go, but they would not produce nearly all the effects desired. The law of primogeniture is a most unrighteous one, but unless the French law of compulsory subdivision of real estate is introduced in its place, its mere abolition would work but little good. The estates of intestates alone would be affected by the change, and so long, at all events, as political power is in the hands of the present landed gentry, the social custom would be sure to triumph over any merely negative law of that kind. So too with the custom of entail. There are motives enough now in existence to make a law rendering it illegal to entail land non-effective through evasions, were it a justifiable law on any reasonable grounds. Behind the land monopoly lies the monopoly of political power, and the great families will fight bitterly to retain that power. The true way to destroy both primogeniture and entail as harmful customs, is to take it out of the power of landowners to maintain with profit the one or the other. Were the elaborate provisions for the out-door relief of the pauperised younger sons of the nobility and gentry which exist in the public services—including therein the Church—to be swept away, I believe the law and habit of primogeniture could not be long maintained. The destruction of the political supremacy of the landlords should, on the other hand, exercise a potent influence in checking entail. The most powerful motive for its continuance would then be withdrawn, and its evil effects might be further neutralised by putting real estate on the same footing as personalty in regard to claims for debt. If the rights of a mortgagee could not be legally barred by an entail, or if the heir to an encumbered estate possessed power to clear off the encumbrances by selling part of his land, all private deeds to the contrary, many properties now steeped in debt would inevitably come to market and be subdivided. Common justice demands such a reform, and were it obtained the owners of land might safely be left to frame entails or not as they pleased. I believe it is not by any means an exaggeration to say that were lands now saleable in payment of debt in the same way as household furniture, one-fourth of the estates in this country might be flung on the market. The extent to which "settlements," the propensity for gambling on the turf, at cards, in every form, and the prevalence of extravagant social vices, have burdened the soil of this country is so great that many seemingly wealthy noblemen and squires are mere hard-up pensioners in the hands of their creditors or trustees. A notorious proof of this was recently furnished by the Duke of Hamilton, and he is only an extreme example of a state of things which prevails the land throughout, in quarters, too, where few would suspect it. Great noblemen who make great show in "society," are often among the most pitiable debt-ridden creatures on the face of the earth. They hold the land in bondage, and are themselves bound to it as by fetters of iron. Therefore the power of such men to destroy the fertility of the soil by loading it with debt, by placing their tenants in slavery, not to themselves, but to creditors and trustees for creditors, ought imperatively to be taken away. No entail should be allowed to interfere with the right of a man's creditors to sell his goods, to "realise his assets," in order to pay themselves, be these assets what they may.

Such changes as these, however, imply a complete upsetment of the basis on which our representative government now rests. So long as the land gives its nominal owners the power to govern the county, so long as English constituencies are content to lick the dust from the feet of squire or landlord who condescends to "represent them in Parliament," or to order—or bribe—them to choose him, just so long will the landowners cling, at all hazards and costs, in spite of unspeakable miseries, to their privileges.

Substantial changes in the law of primogeniture and strict limitations of the power to entail would not in themselves, and in a country like this, do a great deal to subdivide the ownership of land. What one extravagant owner was forced to disgorge his nearest wealthy neighbour, or a new man with much money, would be sure to buy, and things would go on much as before. Nor would the addition of a cheap land registry in every county help matters to a great degree. The monopoly is too all-absorbing in its influence on men's imaginations, the wealth of the land too concentrated to make the competition of small and poor men effective to the extent it would require to be if the soil is to be really distributed. Nay more,—we reason within a circle,—so long as the attention is confined to remedies like these, we may say that true parliamentary reform is impossible while the land remains, or is likely to remain, in few hands. Not even equal electoral districts, manhood suffrage, and paid membership could free the counties from the dominance of the few men with the power of life and death over millions in their hands. The form of corruption only would be changed, its substance would remain.

Therefore it is that if we are to have genuine relief for the nation, genuine liberty to till the soil and to enjoy the fruits of the tillage, we ought logically to be prepared to go much further. The true course for the land reformer is, I think, suggested by the very fact that we have to deal with a natural monopoly as well as by the history of the origin of our land tenures. That history proves that the present overweening power of the small landowning class is the outcome of a fraud on the nation—a fraud and an usurpation. In early times the soil belonged to the people or to the crown, as in a crude and inefficient way the representative of the people. Certain lords, barons, knights, yeomen, and others enjoyed privileges under the crown, or the one of the other, or "in common," and for the good government of the common weal each had his appointed duty; but absolute ownership of the land was enjoyed by none under the king. Gradually, as every student of our history knows, one class in the kingdom has drawn to itself all the rights and privileges pertaining to the ownership or usufruct of landed estate. The peculiarly narrow and cramped basis on which our representative system was framed enabled that class to do this almost with impunity. It inclosed common lands in defiance of the rights of the yeomen and peasantry. It took advantage of feebleness in the monarch to draw to itself rights and privileges vested in the crown —such as the power to tax land or the rights to "royalties" on all minerals found under the land— and gradually concentrated upon itself and its position a kind of halo of sacredness in the possessions thus filched from the people. The blessings of a too mercenary church, alike with the subserviency of a corrupt legal body, were enlisted on the side of the few who held political influence, and in the result we see to-day a few thousand men nominally owning England, and holding its millions under their heel. A sadder, more woe-laden sight the civilized world has not to show.

Surely the first step in any thorough land reform should be for the "crown," the nation, in some way to resume a portion of its rights. The first fruit of the natural monopoly in the land—a monopoly whose value is determined not only by the political privileges it conveys, but by the fact that cultivated land yields rent—ought to belong to the people at large. Therefore the proper way in which to initiate that kind of land reform which is essential to the well-being of the community ought surely to lie in the appropriation of part of the rent for the good of the state. Amongst other overreachings perpetrated by the ruling class on the nation is that of evasion of the burdens of taxation. It is a class which has not scrupled to lay all manner of burdens on the common people, including the charges for our unwieldy debt, contracted in waging many unjust and abominable wars against other nations with whom we had no business to interfere, and against the cause of freedom; but it has shirked its fair share of those burdens. Political economists and statists are often severely exercised to determine the incidence of our clumsy system of taxation, and waste much energy in the bootless dispute. Whether the peasant who smokes his ounce of tobacco per week, paying $2\frac{1}{2}d.$ to the Government therefor, and $\frac{1}{2}d.$ to the tobacco manufacturer, pays more than the gentleman who puffs or gives away a pound of costly cigars in the same time, each contribute to the state dues in proportion to their means, is indeed a most recondite question in the eyes of some, and there is much solemn head-wagging over it. In like manner the problem whether poor, education, or other rates are borne by the occupier or the owner in towns, or by the farmer or landlord in the country, is a very knotty one. You can say much on both sides, and it is always open to a vigorous debater to floor his opponent by flinging at his head Ricardo's famous "theory of rent." How that theory, true, concise, and excellent though it be, applies to the ground landlord in London, who lets the plots to speculative builders for eighty or ninety years, at a fixed rental, it might trouble the rigorous controversialist to say, but the truth of the matter is, that all these discussions are, to a great extent, empty vanities, of no practical moment. They could never have had any existence if the true principle had been all along adopted of putting the taxes directly on the rent—rent being the first gauge of the value of the monopoly. The landlords have avoided this; everything that can possibly be made to do so falls on the occupier, who, if he be a leaseholder, may find his taxation burdens steadily growing, without a corresponding mitigation of rent, and if a tenant-at-will is yet in practically the same position by reason of the difficulty of moving to new localities, should the landlord, as is likely, take no account of the higher taxation. Owing to the burdens being thus for the most part laid on at the wrong end of the scale, the landlords have always the advantage, and there can be no practical doubt that the poor as well as the dependent middle classes have in consequence been most cruelly mulcted. Among all the lower classes in town and country, taxation often seriously pares down the means of subsistence.

Plain justice, therefore, as well as sound economic precept, demands that the nation should retrace its steps and begin at the right end. I see, speaking theoretically, no reason at all why the system which we have applied throughout the North-West Provinces of India and the Punjaub should not work well at home. State rent, subject to periodical revision every thirty years, ought to be levied on the landowner, leaving him to recoup himself out of his tenants if he could, or to give place to those tenants if he could not. In other words, the state ought to claim a fixed portion of the rent of the soil from the present recipients thereof, and in time will probably be driven to do so should these owners remain. As has been already pointed out, such a tax exists now, but it is on a valuation nigh two centuries old, and is merely a monument of the policy of the landowners towards the people. It is, besides, in many instances redeemed. A new tax ought, therefore, to be imposed, and we should then see practically whether the landowner has been bearing his fair share of the national burden or not. Were we to put a tax of 5s. per acre on all arable land bearing 20s. an acre rental now, of 10s. on all bearing 30s. rental, and of 15s. on all bearing 40s. rental, were we to tax game preserves inclosed out of cultivable land at 5l. per acre, and all private parks of more than fifty acres at the average rate of the neighbouring arable land, more would be done to make practicable that free trade in land which Mr. Bright, the late Mr. Kay, and others advocate, than any amount of patching, remedial, or preventive legislation could do. Encumbered estates would then perforce be disentailed and brought to market, and the presence of the land tax in measure commensurate with the nation's necessities would effectually prevent the wealthy from seeking to monopolise the soil. It would fall into the hands of men who would devote themselves to its tillage, and by whom alone its fertility could be increased and the tillage made profitable. No fact is more thoroughly established than the fact that small proprietors make most out of the land. The peasant proprietors of France, Belgium, and Switzerland, of Germany and of our own Channel Islands, are amongst the most diligent, the most contented, the most thrifty and peace-loving, and, withal, the most conservative people on the face of the earth. Wherever you find extreme poverty, sloth, drunkenness, rural misery and degradation of all kinds, there you find also enormous estates in land held by men who enjoy commensurate privileges and immunities. Than this no truth is more firmly established, and that it should be so is the strongest possible condemnation of the present degrading, antiquated, and brutalising land system of England.

Hence, paradoxical as it appears, one may say that the true remedy to begin with—the true way to secure free trade in land—is to appropriate part of the rent of it for the good of the state. This appropriation would have many advantages, besides that of insuring the distribution of the land among small holders, in whose hands it would rapidly increase in value and productiveness. It would enable us, for one thing, to deal with the drink difficulty more effectually than it ever can be dealt with while the government of the country, now so expensive, has to be carried on by means of indirect taxation; it would enable us to further remove restrictions upon our trade intercourse with foreign nations by the remission or reduction of tobacco, tea, wine, and other duties, and for the collection of which, moreover, a most expensive customs service has to be maintained. I believe that 40,000,000*l*. to 50,000,000*l*. a year might easily be raised from the re-diversion of part of the ground rent to the state, whose it is by right, and that through reduction in the Customs and Excise services, easily made after our fiscal laws had been reformed, the expenditure of the country might be brought down to within 10,000,000*l*. of the higher of these two sums, to the unspeakable relief of the people. More than that, this great reform would at once tend to reduce pauperism, by giving scope for the settlement of the people on the land as owners of their holdings under the Crown, and ought thus to pave the way for the total abolition of the poor-law—a law of most iniquitous origin, and probably the most barbaric and debasing in its influence of any ever promulgated in a nominally Christian land.

In order that the soil might the more rapidly pass

into the hands of the cultivators and peasants now sorely impoverished, it would probably be necessary to give them the right of pre-emption, to establish land mortgage banks, somewhat after the model of those in Russia and Prussia. These, however, should be joint-stock enterprises, subject to state regulation and supervision in certain directions only. In Prussia the system pursued under the land law of 1851 was such as to enable the peasants to buy up the proprietors' rights by the payment of annuities. The land-bank paid the price fixed upon to the feudal lords, and gave the peasant immediate possession, he in turn recouping the bank by payments extending over twenty or thirty years, as agreed upon. This system has worked well in Prussia, and would no doubt work here quite as well. Private enterprise would supply the banks, and if the Government fixed the rate of interest, the terms of the advances, the nature of the mortgage to be given to the banks, with some minor points of administration, nothing else would be required.

It may be said that if the state began by taking the rent, or a part of it, to itself, there would be little necessity to establish banks to find the purchase-money for poor tenants. Landlords would be disposed to abandon their land to the first comer who cared to take it and its burden off their hands. But that would by no means be the result. Although the fact that a heavy rent was put upon the soil by the state would instantly drive all encumbered and probably many overgrown estates into the market, the experience of other countries leads us to expect good prices for them. In France forty years' purchase is often paid for small bits of soil, and in this country, with the machinery here sketched in force, thirty to thirty-five years' purchase would probably be easily obtained from the tenants, including the capitalised value of the state rent. Putting that as equivalent to, say, from ten to fifteen years' purchase, the sellers would still get about twenty years' purchase in cash for their lands. That certainly would not be confiscation, and this is probably a moderate estimate. Once secure the freedom of the land from feudal domination and put it in the way of farmers, peasants, and small moneyed men to possess each his own patch or farm, and competition would drive prices up. It has done so in Ireland, and would be likely to do so here, notwithstanding the fact that our peasantry is so reduced and poor.

This then is the first and most important step in any radical transformation of the ownership of the soil. If the land reformers of the country could carry it into effect they would have done a great deed in aid of the redemption of the nation. Of course any hint at such a proposal is always met by a fierce outcry about confiscation, "vested interests," and so forth; but such a cry bears very little honest examination. In the first place, it is surely time for the landlords to make some sacrifice for the nation's good. The nation has long enough laid its life-blood and its first fruits humbly at their feet. There is no scruple made when Government extravagance or the exigencies of petty wars and bantam-cock struttings all over the world cause additions to the people's burdens, to increase the income-tax, or the duties on articles of consumption. Yet these demands are as much acts of confiscation on the poor as an appropriation of part of the inordinate land rent would be on the rich. If I pay 10*l.* a year income tax now as compared with 5*l.* three years ago, my income remaining the same, is not the extra 5*l.* "confiscation" within the landowner's meaning of the word? All taxation, if it come to that, is confiscation, and the only question is, Who ought to have most of it? Which class is best able to bear it, and by its position in the country has the most right to submit for the good of the state? Surely the landowners. Why should capital invested in land be more sacred in the eyes of the Government than any other kind of capital, or than the wages of honest labour? There is no reason for it except in the union of those who own the land and the disorganised, ignorant indifference of the multitude. The "confiscation" cry can however be met on other grounds, *viz.*, that it really would, on the landlords' own interpretation of the word, apply to but few of their number. The great majority of the owners of land in this country have spent comparatively little capital on their possessions, either in purchase or improvement. Some amongst them now enjoy, or ought, if they or their ancestors had been thrifty, to enjoy, incomes probably twice as large as the original capital value of their estates. Those amongst them who have executed improvements have, in a majority of cases, done so chiefly or wholly at the tenants' expense or by state aid, and the movement in their rents has, as a rule, been the outcome of the tenants' labours and self-denial, not theirs. In many other cases that movement is due to causes which are just as much outside either merit or effort on the part of the landowners, such as the extension of towns over agricultural land, the opening of railways, by selling strips of land to whom many a landowner has recouped himself almost, if not altogether, the price of his estate, and the rise in prices due to the prodigious increase in population and wealth. All such causes offer strong justification for, not reason against, the reassertion of the rights of the nation to a share in the direct benefit arising from a natural monopoly which, in strict fairness of principle, as well as legally, belongs to it, and of which it has been defrauded.

The plea of public necessity, however, overrides all others, and it is by no means improbable that if the landowners of England do not give way here, the present artificially degraded position of the masses of the people will before so very long threaten country and landlords alike with ruin. Adversity is a sharp school, and adversity may carry the neglected, ignorant, inarticulate, and hungry masses of this country farther than men dream of one of these days, if the landowners do not step down from their Olympian exclusiveness and be as other men are. Indubitably they do not now bear anything like their fair share of the burdens of the country even as ordinary taxpayers. While such owners of real estate as railway companies, owners and also occupiers, find their mere local assessments year by year creeping up and affording some measure of the growth of public burdens on the people, the landowners' mansions and grounds stand where they did perhaps more than half a century ago. Mr. Inglis Palgrave—whose monograph on local taxation is full of interesting facts and painstaking labour, has moreover proved that the burdens of local assessments are increasing in ratio on the occupier and decreasing on the owner. In towns this cannot but be so under our present system, and the very fact that it is so is "grinding the faces of the poor" to an extent that becomes yearly more fearsome to contemplate. The proportion borne by the mere tenant is not only growing heavier, but the gross amount levied has been steadily mounting up by the increase of expensive habits, of debt charges, and of new channels of expenditure. All the while the land goes untouched, or nearly so. Not even the great endowments founded on it are liberated for the benefit of the community at large. An extremely limited class enjoys the rent it yields, the unearned increment of that rent, and the whole of the social, political, and material advantages which spring therefrom. Assuredly whatever may be the solution of the difficult land problem which this ill-assorted state of affairs has originated, this monstrous unfairness cannot last so very much longer.

There is an alternative "first step" in the emancipation of the soil, which is the favourite remedy with my friend Mr. Barclay, and, failing the tax, it is the one that will probably be adopted by radical reformers. Already, indeed, the farmers are beginning to whisper about it among themselves—in fear and trembling as yet, but with ever-waxing courage. That remedy is fixity of tenure, and it is far more adapted to commend itself to the farmers than the remedy of a heavy land-tax or rent-sharing policy, which is more likely to find favour among the crowded over-taxed masses in the towns. This fixity of tenure means that every landholder, at the date of the passing of the law, should at once become possessed of perpetual rights in his holding, subject only to the payment of a fixed rent to the landlord. At one blow, in short, the landlord would be divorced from the soil except as a perpetual mortgagee. The tenant of whatever class, whether leaseholder or tenant-at-will, would become absolutely possessed of all power over the land—to crop it as he pleased, to plant trees or cut down trees as he pleased, to kill game or preserve it as he pleased, and to sell or sub-let. So long as the rent fixed upon by agreement or valuation was paid by the occupier it would be no business of the holder of the mortgage who that occupier might be. He would have lost absolutely all power over him and over the land he held. This short and summary remedy would at once do away with the necessity for elaborate provisions about "compensation for improvements," with the law of distress, and with all other marks of a miserable feudal bondage, and would effectually prevent the landowner from insidiously exerting his power to compel tenants to contract themselves out of the protection of such laws as there are—a course now too frequently pursued with a contempt for law and order worthy of the great Conservative party. Many landlords, for example, try to protect themselves against possible changes in the game laws by stipulations in their leases, providing that all such changes shall be null and void as between them and their tenants.

Game laws and everything else of the nature of a clog would at once disappear under a perpetual-tenure law, which would convert the present owners into mere rent-receivers or mortgagees. Nor could the landowners urge that such an alteration would mean confiscation, for they at present do nothing for the land in the vast majority of instances except at the occupier's expense. Practically, too, such a law would probably lead to greater subdivision of holdings than now prevails, the so-called "high farming" being excessively costly, and on the whole not the farming calculated in the long run to make the most of the soil, except under extremely favourable conditions. The careful, patient husbandry of the small occupier who labours on his land is the kind of husbandry which makes the earth yield her best increase.

The only solid objection, indeed, that can be urged against this proposal is that it creates a class of people who, without having any defined place in the State, will continue for all time to enjoy incomes which should in great part go to relieve the burdens of the community. The peers and other landowners would, in short, be summarily divorced from the soil and still continue to enjoy its firstfruits. They would also, I suspect, continue to enjoy a preponderance of political influence little calculated to conduce to the public tranquillity or to good government. So many difficult social problems are accumulating for solution, such enormous changes are likely to be brought about by the steady pressure of misery, debt, and current public charges on the people, as well as by the spread of education, that there might be much danger in shutting one class off by itself in the way Mr. Barclay proposes. To that class a real injustice might be done in condemning it to a more objectless life than it now leads. The nation might also suffer. What, for instance, would Mr. Barclay do with the hereditary privileges of the House of Lords? These could not be permitted to remain unaltered after all interest in specially class legislation had been taken away from the lords themselves. Yet were the House of Lords abolished as a self-existing body, the real difficulty would be but one degree lessened. The lords and those commons who owned large fixed rents from land would still constitute the most eligible class from which to draw parliamentary representatives, unless the conditions of representation were so changed that they would not care for the office. If they were also shut off from this occupation, their position would be indeed pitiable. Not even "sport" would be left to them, unless horse-racing were considered sport. Their isolation might thus cause the upspringing of political dangers and social corruptions innumerable. As it is, the landlord class lives under many grave moral disadvantages. Looking at him as he stands apart from the toiling crowd, it has always been a marvel to me, not that the British aristocrat should be often corrupt and debased, a poor trifler or idealess Sybarite, but that he should still have here and there something of the true noble about him. With all his faults, our aristocrat sometimes has a high nobility in him, and a few of his order adorn and stimulate the race by their self-denying manhood. There is a well-defined aspect in which we can look upon them all as the victims of social and political tyranny, not the tyrants, and marvel that they so often surmount their fate.

And if morally such men suffer much injury now, what would they not suffer under Mr. Barclay's law? Considerations like these may have little practical influence on the changes that are impending, but they warn us not to legislate hastily for the benefit of one class as against another class, however highly privileged. The nation itself is pitted against a small class, and no doubt sooner or later that class will have to give way for the sake of the common weal. The very influences which have for generations past made this class so supreme, which have lately caused it to blossom into splendour never before equalled, are helping to prepare the way for a new order of life. On the wisdom and prudence shown by our aristocracy and by the people in facing the changes at hand will depend the future of England. The one thing to be remembered just now is that the farmers alone are no more the nation than the landlords before whom they cringe. Behind both there is a great multitude whose rights, wants, and just aspirations cannot be forgotten.

CHAPTER VII.

THE REMEDIES OF EXPEDIENCY AND COMPROMISE.

THE previous chapter has presented the reader with what may be described as a simple, thorough, and lasting remedy for the present agrarian anomalies of England. Whether a forced subdivision of the soil were brought about by a re-adjustment of taxation, or by the creation of an inalienable tenant-right, a complete revolution in the land customs and laws of England would at once take place. Unhappily, the speedy adoption of simple and effective remedies is as yet by no means easy or probable. Judged by the experience of the past, all great changes in the bases of political power and in social laws can be effected in this country only in a gradual, illogical and clumsy fashion. As has been more than once said, the ideal cure for landlordism, with its accompanying economic drawbacks and social miseries, would probably require as preliminary to its adoption an entire revolution in our representative system, and that cannot be hoped for at any assignable date unless the country, which Heaven forbid, be first caught in the throes of a destructive revolution. There are not the necessary intelligent forces as yet developed in the country to effect it. Our social life is too complex, our people too loosely bound together in moral or political sympathies; there is too much class dominance, ignorant prejudice, and snobbish toadyism bred in the bone to make reform easy. We have therefore to consider how far it may be possible to go in the direction of true reform with the means at command. Will it be possible to do anything, however clumsily, by the aid of existing parliamentary institutions, or must we go on and face an outburst of social commotion?

My impression is that the answer to these questions will depend on circumstances. Those parliamentary institutions of ours will not, of their own motion, help the people in the very least, but they may be impelled to do much if national calamities frighten the lawmakers. What real step towards reform may be taken will be due to the solidarity with which the people are driven, by force of circumstances, to unite to demand reform. So long as the towns are supine through ignorance, cheap food, or comparatively easy circumstances, there will be no true land reform at all, for the landowners will drive or cajole the farmers to take refuge in measures calculated in their imaginations to do good to the landlords alone. But should the towns be impelled by their miseries to seek relief, there may be a certain forward impulse given to the reluctant legislature. Bad harvests, with the accompaniment of ruined tenants and empty farms, may thus do much good.

To carry the ideal reforms ultimately, there could, however, be no better help than a step or two backward. The return to protection all round would probably act like magic in rousing the masses to make a clean sweep of all barbaric laws relating to land and drink and the poor. Perhaps the landowners and manufacturers may, after all, be too shrewd to risk danger in this way. Their present vapourings may die away when practical effect has to be given to their selfish policy. One dare not predict. But practical English reformers must calculate on the prudence of the ruling classes when the crisis comes, for it has never long deserted them in the past, and has been the means of conserving their position time and again at critical periods in our history. To the practical workaday world reformer the question of the land laws therefore presents itself in a somewhat different shape than to the idealist. He has to ask not what ought to be done, but what can be done in existing circumstances, and with the actual tools to hand. He may not see his way to get anything like what is wanted, but must be content to proceed step by step.

Herein lies the value of the proposals of such men as the late Mr. Kay and other advocates of free trade in land. They do not afford the true and abiding remedy, and certainly do not secure "free trade" in land; but they present something that seems practicable to the compromise-loving, vested-interest-worshipping English mind. And already we find the more enlightened amongst the landowning class seizing on some of these proposals as indicating for them a way of salvation. Thus Lord Airlie, in the valuable essay already quoted, puts down among the reforms which he is willing to see carried out the abolition of the laws of hypothec and distraint, and the partial, if not complete, abolition of the custom of entail. He would also provide for the better registration of landed property so as to facilitate its sale, although he does not think that such a change would lead to the subdivision of the land among a multitude of small owners. His reason for so thinking is not based on lack of men able to buy, but on economic grounds; for the man who rents land, he declares, makes more money out of the land than the man who owns. It is not my business to dispute this point with him, nor does it need disputing, for all experience in countries where the soil is owned by small proprietors is dead against his conclusion. What concerns me is the light which such, on the whole, liberal views as these throw on the land reformer's path. If he works along the lines thus indicated he will work on the lines of least resistance, and gain something of his object. This view is strongly confirmed by the observations of Lord Hartington in the debate on Mr. Chaplin's motion for the appointment of a Commission on agriculture. The speech which the leader of the Opposition then delivered has attracted far less attention than it deserved. The concluding portion of it in particular is so striking that I cannot refrain from quoting it:—

"And now let us see," he says, "what the system is which is advocated by hon. gentlemen on the other side of the House. It is not one ordained by any natural law, nor is it one which exists, so far as I know, in any other country in the world. It is a system which exists where the land is divided into large estates, and where the proprietors, though wealthy men, are often not complete masters of their own property, and not able to deal with it as they may desire. It is a system under which the cultivation of the soil is carried on by a class of men who are not the owners of the soil, and not the actual cultivators of the soil; and under which the actual cultivators of the soil are never and can never hope to become its owners. It is a system under which the land is cultivated by men who have this one claim upon it—that in case of old age or absolute destitution they should be supported without expense and almost without labour on the land. Such is the land system of this country, and, as I have said, it is one which prevails in no other country in the world. But I may be asked—Why call attention to the fact? My answer is that it is you who do so, who ask for a Royal Commission to inquire into the condition of agriculture under this system, and who are hinting at what is, in my opinion, the wildest and most radical and revolutionary remedy which could be proposed for the depression of which you complain —a tax on the food of the entire people. I am not saying that this is a system which it is necessary to abolish. I am not contending that it is not a system which may be best suited to the circumstances of the country, but I do say that it is a system which is remarkable, and one which in its results has been so impeached to-night by hon. gentlemen opposite as to be deserving of investigation. I believe that this system is overlaid by conditions, and that there are blots which are not intentional in the system, which are capable of being amended, and which ought to be amended if this system is to be continued with advantage to the community. I cannot at this hour of the night go into the details which have been ably presented to the House, but I will make one or two observations. I believe that one of these blots—one at all events which deserves the most careful and the fullest inquiry—is our system of entail and settlement of land. I hope that in saying that I shall not be regarded as saying anything very radical, even by hon. gentlemen opposite. I think they, who have a practical knowledge of these things, would be the first to admit that there are duties which ought to be discharged by the owner of a large estate. But what if the owner of a large estate has not even the inclination to discharge those duties? Is it to the advantage of the land, is it to the advantage of himself, of his tenants, of the labourers on his estate, of the whole community that that man should by any artificial system be forced to remain in a position which he does not desire to occupy in consequence of conditions which were imposed 50, 60, or 100 years ago, and of which he cannot get rid? I omit altogether the consideration of the Act of Parliament which enables limited owners to charge their estates with the cost of the improvement of estates. I doubt very much whether any palliative of this kind can altogether override the effect of that system, which gives only a limited and life estate to a man. At all events, I have very strong authority for saying that up to a very short time ago this Act had produced very small results. Not long ago a committee of the House of Lords, which was presided over by Lord Salisbury, and composed mainly of large landed proprietors, reported on this very subject, and they stated that only a very small fraction of persons interested in land had availed themselves of the provisions of the Act. I think I heard the member for North Norfolk say to-night that the conclusions of that Committee are altogether worthless. I can only wonder that such an expression should have been used with reference to a Committee of the House of Lords presided over by so eminent a statesman and so large a landowner as Lord Salisbury. Well, something was said about the question of small proprietors. I hope I am not going to be too radical on this subject. At all events I have the support of the noble lord who has just spoken. The noble lord has expressed as strong a wish as could be expressed by any one that the number of small proprietors should be increased. I do not venture to express any confident opinion whether under our social system arrangements it ever would be possible by any legitimate means to create a large class of small proprietors. It seems not wise to maintain, if you could avoid doing so, a system of law which makes the transfer of land so difficult and so expensive to small proprietors. That, surely, is a fair subject of inquiry. I wish to say one word as to the question of tenants' improvements. Freedom of contract is made the battle-cry, and I am disposed to agree with it. I have always been disposed to look with suspicion on compulsory tenant right from which ever side it may come. I ventured to express this view on the Agricultural Holdings Bill, and I was anxious that the parties should be free to make their own arrangements. Something has been said about the law of distress in England and the corresponding law in Scotland. I will not go into this question at length, but there again is a subject which seems well worthy of inquiry. The law of distress is a question of the ordinary law of debtor and creditor. It is contended, with a considerable show of reason, that this law acts detrimentally not only to the landlords and tenants, but also to every one else who is concerned. I do not wish needlessly to protract this debate, but I do not think there will be any difference on either side that at such an inquiry as is proposed questions of local taxation should be discussed. That is a question which we all recognise most deeply concerns the agricultural interest. I see no just claims for the exemption of the land from burdens which have been acquired or inherited. I say in the case of new burdens there is a case for inquiry; and, speaking for myself, I am perfectly willing to hear what the tenants or landlords have to urge. All these subjects are included in, or are not excluded by, the motion of my hon. friend, the member for Mid-Lincolnshire; but at the same time I am able to see the advantage that is likely to be gained by the House acceding to the motion which has been made, inasmuch as the matter for inquiry must range over a great variety of subjects, and there is a great difference between the powers given to a Parliamentary Committee and the scope of those which are intrusted to a Royal Commission. We ought, therefore, before agreeing to the appointment of a Royal Commission, to understand clearly the nature of the questions which are to be referred, and I hope some explanation on the point will be given by Her Majesty's Government. We on this side of the House greet with the greatest satisfaction the prospect of a full and impartial inquiry into all the causes which affect the agricultural depression, which we, in common with the whole country, so deeply deplore."—*Times report.*

If the reader will bear in mind that these words were uttered by the heir of one of the most princely houses in England, their significance will seem incapable of over-estimation. The germs of almost all that has been asked for in the previous chapter are to be found in this speech, and it lays down the lines on which land reformers may work with luminous precision.

Lord Hartington appears to be at one with the advocates of so-called free trade in land in advising the prohibition or modification of entails. He would render the transfer of land cheap and easy, instead of costly and liable to be tainted by frauds, and he hints at hostility to the existing law of distress. Not content with that, Lord Hartington is bold enough to say that the land might well be made to bear directly a fuller share of the burden of public taxation. True, he ignores the game laws, and is strong on "freedom of contract"; but, heir as he is to a great English dukedom, it must be admitted that he is prepared to grant a great deal that would ameliorate the position of the landholder. His words prove to us that some reform may be possible without revolution—that the warning uttered by Mr. Bright in the stately, impassioned speech delivered by him on the same evening has not been without its effect. Speaking on the startling fact—much dwelt on in these pages—that a few thousand persons own the land of England, he burst forth :—

"The Commission will have to inquire—I tell the hon. gentleman opposite that he has opened the door, and it cannot now be closed—the Commission will have to inquire whence comes this gigantic monopoly —how comes it that the great bulk of the population are thus divorced from the soil of their native land? They will ask how it is that there are these great farms, requiring great capital, which are now most disastrously affected by the distress which so unfortunately prevails. They will ask—and hon. gentlemen opposite should put this question to themselves in all seriousness—how is it that your tenants, as you say, almost universally, but I hope not universally, but locally and partially, are coming to you, owing you twelve months' or six months' rent, and asking you to take 15s. in the pound of the debt they owe you? When these people are in debt to other persons than landowners—say to their saddlers, their farriers, to the dealer from whom they buy manures or the utensils used in farming—they would not dare to go to them and ask them to accept 15s. in the pound in satisfaction of their debts. That would bring them into liquidation or bankruptcy. But such is their position, with regard to the landowners, that they ask you to take 15s. in the pound as that which they owe you. And many of you—some because you cannot help it, but a great number, I have no doubt, from sympathy and generosity and kindness

—make these concessions to your tenants. But I confess there is to me something terrible in the idea that hundreds of thousands of tenant farmers throughout Great Britain—many of them, if you see them, as much gentlemen as the landowners themselves; they live in good houses, they keep hunters, and they educate their children as well as their means permit—should be so humiliated—for that is what they would call it in Lancashire—as to ask somebody to whom they owe 100*l.* as a just and lawful debt to take 75*l.* instead of the 100*l.* That is the state of things in this great, paramount interest which you represent; and somehow you are blind. You don't open your eyes to the fact; so usual with you is this extraordinary thing, you don't appear to regard it as anything of any great consequence when it periodically happens just for a time. . . . . Let the Commission inquire, if it can, how it comes that the landowners of this country and the farmers are looking, not only with alarm, but with terror, to the trade in corn and in cattle which have to be brought from a distance of 3,000 or 4,000 miles across the Atlantic. That is a question which they may fairly examine."

Well, Lord Hartington at all events professes himself willing to investigate the problem with a view to amendment, and it is a good augury. The people have but to nerve themselves and stick to their demands for the liberation of the land, and in some form they will be obeyed. Complete reform may not be possible. At first only a clumsy, disjointed, hardly workable kind of reform may be granted or hoped for. But work well begun is half done, they say, and the momentum of a crowded and needy population is sure to hurry the country forward faster and faster in the required direction. We shall pass from carefully-guarded concessions, yielded as sops to popular necessities, to the fully-acknowledged rights of the people to share in the wealth of the soil, and ultimately, I trust, reach that best ideal of landownership which is embodied in its distribution among a multitude of free cultivators forced only to contribute out of the firstfruits of their monopoly to the demands of the commonwealth.

On this practical side of the subject little more need be said. The course to be followed is, in the main, to take the landlords' concessions and press them home. This course may be roundabout and clumsy, but it promises, I think, to lead to success by a more sure and peaceable way than any other—if only there be time! A few more seasons like the present would hurry us into revolution. We may hope for a better fate; and trusting that time for reform, in the slow, illogical, English way, will be given, it will now be well to indicate briefly what the principal points in any land-law reform worthy the name must be. On the most moderate view of the necessities of the people, the land reformer must demand at least these following concessions and emancipations :—

I. Modification of the custom of entail, so as to permit encumbered owners to sell for their own relief, or bankrupt owners to be sold up for their creditors' satisfaction.

II. The abolition of the law of primogeniture, and the placing of real and personal estate on precisely the same footing in the eyes of the law.

III. The repeal of the right of distraint and the law of hypothec in a manner so effectual as to place the landlord on precisely the same footing as the ordinary creditor, neither higher nor lower.

IV. The institution of a cheap and thoroughly efficient system of registration of titles in every county in the kingdom, so that the buyer of land could, on payment of a small fee, at once ascertain the condition of the property bought, its encumbrances, and the nature of the title of the seller—all mortgages or settlements on land not indexed in the registry being of course debarred their rights as against a purchaser.

V. The abolition of the landlord's game monopoly by a law vesting all rights to the ground vermin and winged game on the land in the cultivator. A law of this kind to be effective, however, must be accompanied by such modifications in the trespass laws as would materially reduce the power of magistrates to punish persons, either by fine or imprisonment, when caught on ground not their own. The unpaid magistracy ought, however, to be abolished altogether.

VI. In the tenant's behalf, and as a protection for his capital, the least reform which can be tolerated is a law giving him absolute security for all improvements effected on the soil or buildings of his farm, perfect liberty of cropping and to dispose of his crops, and security against arbitrary re-valuations of his holding for at least twenty years. That is the term fixed by an enlightened landlord, the Earl of Leicester,[1] and it is the shortest term tolerable. Without that proviso, moreover, the tenant could have little or no security in any "tenant-rights" clause, for a grasping landlord might always, by capricious re-valuations, draw the profits of the tenant's expenditure to himself.

VII. These reforms would not be complete without the institution of an encumbered estates court, and

---

[1] See Mr. W. Howard's pamphlets, *Impediments to the Development of British Husbandry*, Rowland Hill and Sons, Bedford; and *The Tenant Farmer: Land Laws and Landlords*, Macmillan and Co.

without a law bestowing the right of pre-emption on the tenants of estates brought under the administration of that court. The abolition of primogeniture and reduction of the privileges of landowners to a point that would both allow and compel them to part with portions of their land in order to pay their debts, would be the means in time of throwing probably fully one-half the land of the United Kingdom into the market. In present circumstances that land might be bought by small owners on comparatively favourable terms; but conditions might easily arise, and no doubt would arise, so long as political power and territorial possession hang together, wherein the competition of the small farmer would be ineffective as against the large capitalist. He should, therefore, have the right of pre-emption; and to enable him to exercise that right the land banks already mentioned might be established, or power given to the insurance companies to act as such by lending farmers the necessary capital, repayable by annuities. Some such machinery is needed here under any scheme of land reform, else the people will not readily get back the possession of the soil.

These briefly are the leading features in the "reforms of expediency." In the end they come to much the same as the more sweeping measures which would secure complete, absolute, and inalienable tenant-right to occupiers, or which would, by the appropriation of part of the rent of the land for the benefit of the State, compel an instant redistribution of the soil. But though the ends are the same, the clumsier and more roundabout method of reform is probably the one most likely to be adopted. It can be obtained bit by bit; it permits of compromises, of concessions that serve to hide surrenders; the moneyed interests of the landowning class are less obviously interfered with; and rough, practical concrete aims are presented to the popular mind in a way that it can grasp.

Whatever course is followed, the task will be no light one. Thus far, as Mr. James Howard very truly says, the little band of land-law reformers in their efforts to bring about needful changes have received but little aid from popular support, whilst they have had to contend with the opposition of the most powerful, the most wealthy, and the most influential class of the community.[1] This apathy is born of ignorance, of that habit of bondage which many generations have bred in the bone. The people do not know and never suspect that the land-laws of England are the cause of more than half their

[1] *The Tenant Farmer*, &c., p. 7.

misery; that to these laws they owe it that their children ofttimes can find neither rest nor bread in their native land, are swept off the soil into the unwholesome slums of our great centres of industry in numbers so great that the competition for existence there is fast becoming an unbearable life-long agony. The middle classes are almost as blind and ignorant as the lower, and their consequent apathy is something that makes the land-law reformer's heart sink within him, not merely because he gets no support, but because the apathy may be so incalculably dangerous in times of national crises.

Hitherto the landlords have taken advantage of the stupidity of the people, and as they have done they will continue to do, unless the public be somehow awakened. The mass of the landlords, too, are so wedded to the existing order of things as to be utterly blind to their own pecuniary interest—how much more to the dangers that lie before them. Were they but wise, they would eagerly lead in the path of reform, eagerly obtain power to sell portions of their entailed, and too often encumbered, estates, of their own accord afford every facility to men of enterprise, capital, and skill, to peasant and yeoman, to devote their money and energy to the tillage of the soil. That course would be their own salvation and a means of adding to their wealth and power. But all, save an intelligent and far-seeing minority, will resist, will try to impose fresh burdens on the nation, rather than take off some of those it now groans under, and in doing so may pave the way for a very summary reform some day. Should reform in some shape be denied now, a day will assuredly come when all theories of reform, all partial, temporising measures will be swept away by the blind, mad rush of an infuriated, tax-ground, hungry people. I earnestly advise the landowners of this country not to court *that* alternative. There will be no nice distinctions of property rights when the angry passions of a hungry, ignorant people unite them with one fell purpose. Our country is full of what may be called the primary elements of revolution, and they might develop themselves with the devastatory rapidity of a tropical storm under easily conceivable conditions. A few more years of dull trade, a continuance of the declining yield of the soil, the advent of new troubles in India or in Eastern Europe involving us in a costly and bloody war, or the temporary bankruptcy of a few of our colonies,—any one of these not improbable events might be sufficient to precipitate the avalanche whose fall would sweep land-system and landlords at once out of existence. The resisting privileged class forgets that an increased population introduces, by itself alone, an element of danger which cannot be ignored. Lord Derby serenely advises the discontented to emigrate; but there are not two millions of people in the United Kingdom who at the present moment could afford to take his advice, however willing, whatever hope other lands might afford them; and what is two millions among so many? Shall we export our paupers, or whom? Where could masses of people find work and food were they to go, and how would it fare with the solitary grandees left behind in their penniless, barren-acred glory? This recipe, manifestly, will not do. Game would not sustain the country. No temporising, no ostrich oblivion, no playing with the edge tools of sham concessions can answer long, and the sooner Lord Derby and his class recognises the fact the better. The new generation will not go in the steps of that passing away. Those very industrial forces which the new "iron age" has evoked push us steadily towards changes in the modes of our national existence which may turn out to be chaotic if the ablest, most enduring, and most freedom-stifling knot of "obstructives" that the world has ever known since the days of the old Roman senate do not have a care and give way in time.

Meanwhile the Radical party must not be disheartened. An impression has already been made in the ranks of the landowners, and for some years to come fear and threatened or actual poverty are likely to be the great allies of the land-reformers. Let them press on steadily with practical aims, content to take what is expedient sometimes, instead of that which is best, and the end will be attained. If they work well and with a will, they may yet save the nation from destruction and the landlords from themselves.

POSTSCRIPT.

SINCE the preceding pages were written, for the most part early in the present year, several superficial changes have taken place in the aspect of affairs. Trade has, it is said, revived, silver has so far increased in price that the bimetallist prophets have grown less clamorous, and, last of all, the land law reform agitation has received adherents, and, in Ireland at least, entered on phases little anticipated.

The fact that as regards trade prospects the country is now in a more cheerful mood, may seem to suggest that much written in the time of gloom should be modified; but on full consideration I decided to make no change. Lessons of caution and sobriety are needed now as much as when every one's heart was melting with dread. I am not sure that they are not even more needed, for I doubt greatly the quality of this trade revival. The doubt will seem reasonable when it is considered that in this instance speculation, instead of following, has certainly preceded or outrun the "revival" of genuine demand. Europe, and particularly France and England, are much more dependent on foreign supplies of food this winter than last, and the United States are in the position to take full advantage of this dependence. In consequence of this the States find themselves greatly enriched by what we pay them for food, and they have begun to buy recklessly. Prices have risen there until that state of things has come about so much insisted on in the first chapter of this book. The tariff is now no barrier to imports, and the States are once more great buyers in Europe, and especially in England. Again, the action of the Indian Government in Afghanistan has increased Indian orders for railway materials to a very marked extent. These orders have been distributed with judicious care in the chief centres of industry at home, and have helped to "revive trade." Some of our Colonies are likewise large borrowers in aid of "public works," New Zealand, the other day, taking 5,000,000*l*. These changes all indicate more business, and they have produced feverish activity in various directions, most notably in shipbuilding.

But all this and much more would not constitute the basis for such a trade revival as might lift the industries of England up to a level of prosperity as high as that reached in the period preceding 1873. The basis is not broad enough. We are poorer at home now than we have been for very many years, food is dearer, the agricultural interest is much depressed, and therefore the consuming power of the people is much less. This is shown in the customs and excise returns, and while this state of things exists there can be no solid or lasting improvement in the home trade. Speculation will for a few days or months cast a glamour over markets, but if the ultimate consumer do not in time step in to buy, these markets must sink again into a worse stagnation than the first. We have no evidence that the home consumer is coming forward as a greater buyer, nor is there any sign that any country other than those indicated is prepared to take greater quantities of our goods. Our pig-iron even, about the demand for which so much has been said, is already being produced in excess of requirement, and stocks are therefore accumulating. And no wonder, since no European country is able to buy from us with the freedom of past years. What with costly wars and almost as costly preparations for war, what with bad harvests, social disorders, growing poverty, and corrupt governments, there is not a nation in Europe able to become our customers to a greater extent next year than in any of the last five, unless we lend them the money to pay for our goods. It is against all reason to suppose that nations will buy more when they are suffering from increased poverty than when they are comparatively rich.

The same observations apply to countries forth of Europe. What South American state, for instance, is capable of doing a much larger trade with us now than last year? They are all poor, many of them are bankrupt, and some have been exhausting themselves in war. If they are to buy we must lend them the means. And it is the same with the East. It will be urged that prices have risen for their produce, and that therefore they are richer—they can barter more freely; but prices have risen here too, and this advantage is therefore neutralised. In short, except by the old way of foreign loans, inflated credit, and general recklessness, I see no means by which our trade is to enter on that new field of expansion now so much spoken of. The lesson I have sought to enforce must, therefore, stand unaltered, and the anticipations too. I am, indeed, no believer in romances of statistics, and regard the purrings of admiration continually indulged in about our marvellous wealth and power, our over-mastering resources, and so forth, with a certain amazement. If the strength of a chain is measured by its weakest link, surely the wealth of a nation may likewise be known by the adversity-bearing capacity of the lower orders, and England, great wealthy England has more inhabitants either absolute paupers or hovering on the confines of pauperism than any country of equal civilisation on earth. These help not trade revivals, neither does the distress of the genteel classes, wrestling with bills of sale, mortgages, and every description of debt.

Permit me, finally, to draw attention to the evidence now visible on all hands that the great land question is coming to the front. We shall be converted to land reform "through our stomachs." The landowners are of course crying out where the shoe pinches them. With Lord Carington, than whom they have had no better or more outspoken representative, many are now beginning to say that the time has come for inquiring whether it is right that estates heavily mortgaged should be left tied up in such a manner that escape from debt is rendered impossible, and whether the system of land transfer should not be cheapened and simplified. Mr. Gladstone, Mr. Forster, and other members of the last Liberal Government may be classed as adherents to the narrow platform of change which such questions present. But there are other classes who go further. The farmers are drawing together, and their "Alliance," lately formed under the leadership of Mr. Jas. Howard of Bedford, Mr. Jas. W. Barclay, M.P. for Forfarshire, Mr. W. B. Bear, and others well known in agricultural circles, promises to cause no little trouble to Tory candidates at future elections. These farmers will have their views to express about game, about improvements and security for capital, widening thereby the range of coming reform. Reform, however, will not come any the sooner in England for the "agitations" of men like Mr. Parnell in Ireland. He furnishes more reactionary arguments to Tories in England, and does more to cripple the march of true Liberalism than its bitterest professed enemies. His policy is to set class against class, his cry of "no rents" is the cry of one who would set the necessities of the poor above national unity, and the good of a class above the paramount claims of a whole people. Rent cannot be abolished by popular clamour. It must be paid to somebody, or enjoyed by some class, if not appropriated to the good of the nation; and it is poor patriotism to hound on the people against those who, the nation having put forth no claim to its abstract and natural rights, have the only legal claim to this rent. The very fact that I hold the claims of the nation to be paramount compels me to object to the policy of Mr. Parnell, and to lament over his agitation as the most serious present drawback to the progress of real land-law reform.

THE END.

www.ingramcontent.com/pod-product-compliance
Lightning Source LLC
Chambersburg PA
CBHW031349230426
43670CB00006B/480